CW00460448

How to Be Funny

How You Can Make People Laugh Using Secret Humor Techniques, Proven Jokes, and Be Witty Even If You're Not

Free Bonus from Andy Gardner

Hi!

My name is Andy Gardner, and first off, I want to THANK YOU for reading my book.

Now you have a chance to join my exclusive email list related to human psychology and self-development so you can get the ebook below for free as well as the potential to get more ebooks for free! Simply click the link below to join.

P.S. Remember that it's 100% free to join the list.

Access your free bonuses here:
https://livetolearn.lpages.co/andy-gardner-how-to-be-funny-paperback/

Table of Contents

INTRODUCTION 1

CHAPTER 1: THE MOST IMPORTANT FIRST STEP TO LEARNING
HOW TO BE FUNNY...3

CHAPTER 2: THE POWER OF LAUGHING... AT YOURSELF!.....................13

CHAPTER 3: HOW TO GRAB ANYONE'S ATTENTION 22

CHAPTER 4: THE THREE CS: HOW TO BE CHILL, COMFORTABLE,
AND CONFIDENT WHEN TELLING A JOKE...33

CHAPTER 5: THE IMPORTANCE OF TIMING AND TONE 42

CHAPTER 6: BODY LANGUAGE HACKS FOR FUNNY FOLKS 52

CHAPTER 7: THE GOLDEN KEY TO AN UNFORGETTABLE JOKE..........61

CHAPTER 8: PROVEN JOKES THAT WILL MAKE ANYONE LAUGH........71

CHAPTER 9: WONDROUS WAYS TO ENHANCE YOUR WIT... JOKES
ASIDE..83

BONUS: THE JOKESTER'S CHECKLIST 92

CONCLUSION..98

HERE'S ANOTHER BOOK BY ANDY GARDNER THAT YOU MIGHT
LIKE 100

FREE BONUS FROM ANDY GARDNER...101

REFERENCES...102

Introduction

Humor always affects you in some way. It helps you forgive your mistakes faster and view the world with clearer eyes. Comedians are regarded as some of the most intelligent individuals as they must gauge an audience's reaction and time their delivery accordingly. They understand which kinds of comedy are appropriate for which situations. It follows that they're not oblivious to the evils that exist in the world, but they prefer a lighter perspective on life, which they infuse into their inner thoughts and dealings with others.

This book will take average folks like you and me and show us how to be funnier. Charisma is real, you know; it's a popular topic of conversation. Some individuals are naturally charismatic. That is an undeniable truth. However, everything worth doing can be learned. You don't have to make up a personality; we can always find humor inside ourselves.

This book aims to help readers improve their interpersonal relationships by intentionally using humor in conversation. Conversational comedy is more sophisticated than simple setups and catchphrases. Leave the planned jokes to the comedians. Instead, devote your cognitive resources to learning and memorizing skills that may be used effortlessly in ordinary social settings.

The good news is that you'll like the humor in this book and find some of the anecdotes amusing. However, that's the problem with humor; *a cookie-cutter approach simply doesn't work.*

You don't have to hone every skill, but you should focus on the ones that will improve your life and make you laugh. You could even push yourself a little beyond your comfort zone. Once you've mastered one method, it'll be as automatic as swinging a bat, freeing your mind to concentrate on other matters. Practice with people you feel more at ease with, like family or strangers you won't see again. Make small talk with everyone in customer service since they are paid to speak to you!

Knowing your audience, the context, and the emotional climate can help you target your jokes far more precisely and boost your chances of success. You shouldn't always quit if your witty remark doesn't go anywhere the first time - the same hilarious phrase might fall flat with one individual and hit gold with another.

Try not to throw in the towel before things have been seen through to their completion; don't lose steam, slow down, or give up. Remember that the joke will land with the intended audience more effectively if you play along with the hilarity. Audiences can sense when you're trying too hard to be taken seriously or acting as if what you're saying isn't humorous.

As a general principle, avoid using rude or nasty humor. Arrogant or malicious humor may insult rather than delight. Everyone needs more laughter - there is already enough grief in the world.

How would you add some fun to daily life? There isn't a single set method, and this book has all the answers. There is no comedy track. It's all about your ability to make other people laugh. Nothing else matters.

Chapter 1: The Most Important First Step to Learning How to Be Funny

Humor can connect us with others, make us laugh, and spice up our daily lives. As much as we all want to be funny and make people laugh, it isn't always easy. That's why, right now, we're going to take the time to learn some of the fundamental principles of being funny.

In this chapter, you'll learn the most crucial first step to learning how to be funny. You'll learn what separates the pros from the amateurs and how you, too, can join their ranks. Ready to start? Let's dive in!

The Most Crucial First Step: Listen

When it comes to developing the skill of being funny, one rule overrides all the others: **Listen.** Listen to the people around you, pay attention to what makes them laugh, and take note of their reactions. Listen carefully to the words they use and how they tell their stories. Listen to the different inflections in their voices, and note how these can change when someone is telling a joke. Listen to the jokes that make others laugh, and note what makes them funny.

Being a good listener allows you to understand what people find funny and entertaining.
https://www.pexels.com/photo/photo-of-women-talking-while-sitting-3182808/

As you listen and observe, you will learn the craft of storytelling and how to construct your jokes. This skill is essential in being funny because it gives you the foundation to create something funny.

Storytelling is an art that has been around since the dawn of time. Whether sharing tales through the spoken word or writing, it has greatly impacted our shared culture and history. But what does it take to make a good storyteller? Is there a secret formula that makes someone funny? While there are no easy answers to these questions, there is one key element that all good storytellers have in common: they all listen carefully to other people's stories.

Listening is an essential first step to being funny. Listen to the stories around you, pay attention to what makes people laugh, and take note of their reactions. Listen to the words they use and the inflections in their voices. Listen to the jokes that make others laugh, and note what makes them funny.

Listening can be the difference between an average – or even bad – performance and an inspiring and hilarious one. Listening isn't just about understanding the words. It's about truly comprehending and feeling what another person is trying to communicate. This chapter will examine why listening is crucial in "learning funny" and how it can help you develop your witty side. It provides tips and tricks to take note of while listening and ways to apply what you learn in your storytelling.

Unlock your Creativity through Active Listening

Having a good ear for what's funny is essential to being funny. By listening, you can pick up on subtleties that make jokes more interesting and entertaining. When someone tells a story, they often include idiosyncrasies or details that add humor or depth to their tales. By paying attention to these elements, you can understand the nuances of humor and how it works in a story.

Mastering the Art of Timing with Listening

Humor is all about timing, and it's essential to recognize the right moments to deliver a joke or funny story. Timing is key in storytelling – if you don't have the perfect moment for your punchline, your story won't have the desired effect.

Listening helps you identify what is being said by others, when they're saying it, and how it's being said. You become more aware of the conversation and can pick up on subtle cues that mark certain moments as the perfect time to introduce a joke or funny story.

The more you practice your listening skills, the better you'll recognize these moments and time your jokes accordingly. When trying to make an audience laugh, you can use this skill to pick up on the group's mood and energy and understand what kind of jokes or stories work better.

Finally, listening helps build empathy, an essential skill for telling funny stories. Understanding other people's experiences and perspectives allows you to draw on those experiences in your own stories. It will give them more depth and make them more relatable to your audience.

How Can a Person Become a Better Listener?

Listening isn't just about hearing the words. It's about truly understanding their message. It involves paying close attention to how people tell their stories and tuning into body language and facial expressions. Reading between the lines involves catching jokes or puns hidden among the words spoken. All of this can help you decipher the meaning and intent of the storyteller more effectively.

1. The Art of Being Aware and Present

Being present and mindful in the moment is essential for effective listening and successful storytelling. When you're aware of your surroundings and paying attention to small details, you can pick up on subtle elements that could enhance your stories.

Focus on the Moment and Take in the Story Being Told

One of the essential aspects of being a good listener is staying present in the moment. An attentive person listens to the other person's words without letting their mind wander to other topics or conversations. When you stay focused and pay attention, you can pick up on the intricacies of the story, which will help you better understand and apply the same technique to your storytelling.

For example, if someone talks about their experience at an art gallery they recently visited, pay attention to how they describe the paintings or sculptures they found interesting. By taking in these details, you'll understand better why they found the art so captivating and give you ideas for future storytelling.

Tune into Yourself – Pay Attention to Your Reactions and Emotions

Another vital component of being a good listener is understanding your own reactions and emotions. Listen to how the story makes you feel; this can help you recognize certain funny or insightful elements. This way, you can tap into a deeper understanding when engaging with the person telling the story.

If someone shares a funny anecdote about their childhood, pay attention to how it makes you feel. Are you laughing along with them? Are you feeling thoughtful and contemplative? Focusing on your reactions can help you connect to the story more meaningfully.

Remain Objective, Yet Open to New Ideas or Perspectives

It's crucial to remain objective when listening to another person's story. Avoid getting too hung up on the details and instead look at the bigger picture. This helps you recognize certain patterns or themes the storyteller tries to convey.

At the same time, it's good to be open-minded when hearing another person's story. Respect their perspective, and take your time to judge. You find yourself inspired by their experience or learn something new that can help you in your own life.

2. Being Polite and Open

The ability to spin a captivating yarn from the mundane is an art form. It's what makes us laugh, cry, and want to hear more, but it takes practice. Being polite and open to a speaker's message is key to understanding, appreciating, and creating your own stories.

Respect the Speaker's Message

It is necessary to listen with an open mind, no matter how mundane the subject initially seems.

By respecting the speaker's message, you validate their thoughts and ideas. For example, suppose a colleague were to speak about an experience from their past that is irrelevant to the current conversation. In that case, it is essential to listen to and acknowledge their story. This encourages them to keep speaking openly and honestly, leading them deeper into meaningful conversations.

You do not need to necessarily agree with the speaker's message. Still, by responding politely and respectfully, you can show that you are open to hearing what they say.

Do Not Be Afraid to Ask Questions

Asking questions can guide the conversation in a more constructive direction. It can be beneficial to understand what is being said and get clarity on certain topics.

Questions are valuable as they show that you are engaged and interested in what is being discussed while offering an opportunity to dive deeper into the topic. That said, try to avoid asking questions that could be perceived as condescending or leading.

Avoid Being Judgmental or Argumentative

It is easy to offer opposing views or judgments when disagreeing with a speaker's opinion. However, it is essential to remain mindful of the other person's feelings and avoid being overly judgmental. Rather than putting the person on the defensive, focus on understanding their perspective and looking for solutions to any potential issues. Be open to hearing them out and allow them the space to express themselves without feeling judged or attacked.

It can be hard not to get drawn into an argumentative exchange, but keeping a level head will help you maintain a constructive dialogue. Instead of becoming combative, keep the conversation focused on finding a solution or compromise that both parties can agree upon.

Making thoughtful and respectful dialogues will ultimately lead to more productive conversations and better relationships with those around you. Remember to stay open-minded when engaging in conversations. Even if it's difficult to agree, try to remain civil and avoid making judgmental or argumentative statements.

3. Analyze Body Language for Clues

Another integral aspect of being a good listener is paying attention to body language. Look for subtle cues and gestures, such as hand movements or facial expressions. These can tell you a lot about the speaker's emotions and intentions, which can help you better understand what they are trying to convey.

For example, if someone is angry or frustrated, their body posture becomes more rigid or tense. Or, if the speaker is telling an exciting story, they use exaggerated hand gestures or direct eye contact with the listener.

Learn to analyze body language for clues.
https://www.pexels.com/photo/happy-multiethnic-couple-drinking-coffee-and-showing-like-gesture-4245930/

It helps to learn about commonly used gestures in storytelling or comedy. For instance, a shrug of the shoulders might express uncertainty, while a wave of the arm could indicate a sweeping gesture. Learning to interpret body language can enhance your listening skills and help you better understand what is being said.

Last but not least, it is essential to remember that every person expresses their emotions differently. Be aware of other people's cultural backgrounds and biases when interpreting another person's body language. By being aware of these subtle cues, you can gain insight into the speaker's true emotions and intentions and become a better listener.

4. Ignite Creativity by Reading

Reading is one of the best ways to hone your listening skills and gain more knowledge. Engaging with stories through reading can be an incredibly powerful way to kick-start your creativity.

Reading expands your vocabulary and understanding of the world, which can help you become a better listener. It allows you to explore different perspectives that might not be present in your everyday conversations. This can help you develop empathy for other people's experiences and opinions, an essential communication skill.

Learn from Different Narratives

No matter the genre, reading can be an amazing way to open your mind and better understand different narratives. Getting lost in the story is easy when you read, allowing for more meaningful conversations with others.

Reading also helps to build empathy as it allows you to understand other people's struggles and experiences from a unique perspective. It can give you an insight into how different cultures and societies interact. This understanding makes conversing with people from various backgrounds or perspectives easier.

Engage Your Imagination

The art of storytelling helps engage your imagination and creativity. When you read, it is easier to visualize the scene, which can inspire future ideas or conversations. It allows you to make connections between different stories and gain a better understanding of certain topics.

For instance, if you are reading about a character in a book who has experienced a difficult situation, you can use that knowledge to relate with someone going through a similar experience. This helps strengthen empathy and understanding when engaging with others.

Make sure to practice engaging with the narrative rather than passively consuming it. Imagine yourself as part of it – what would you do differently? What kind of conversations would you have with the characters? This will help you become more creative and think outside the box.

Challenge Your Thinking

Reading helps to challenge your existing beliefs and encourages critical thinking. By engaging with different perspectives, it is easier to recognize potential biases and assumptions that you have had. This can help to build better listening skills and knowledge as it allows you to consider multiple viewpoints – and ultimately make more informed decisions.

One of the best ways to engage with reading and hone your listening skills is by joining a book club or discussion group. Being in an environment where people discuss different topics or stories can be incredibly powerful as you learn how different people interpret the same narrative. Reaching out to others and hearing their point of view can help you develop a more well-rounded understanding.

5. Writing Down What Works and What Does Not

Writing down what works when listening will help you hone your storytelling skills and better understand how to communicate effectively with others.

Take Notes on What Works

Pay attention when someone relays a story or anecdote, and jot down all the details that stand out. If the person is particularly expressive in their delivery, write it down so you can emulate that behavior in your own stories.

If they use a lot of descriptive details, make sure to jot those down as well. Taking notes on what works will give you plenty of material to draw from when crafting your tales and help you develop better techniques for storytelling.

Keep Track of Interesting Stories

Whenever you come across a particularly interesting story, be sure to keep track of it. Write down the details, where you heard it, and what made it stand out, so you have it for future reference.

You can look up the story online and see if there are any variations or additions to help make your retelling even more engaging. Keeping track of interesting stories will make developing ideas for your tales easier and more captivating.

Document Ideas for Improvement

If you struggle with a particular part of storytelling, document it so you can refer to it later. Jot down tips or advice that you come across, funny stories that make you laugh, or techniques that can be used to help improve your storytelling skills.

A collection of ideas will give you something to draw from when crafting stories and make it easier to create more captivating narratives.

Humor is essential to storytelling; funny stories can be the most memorable. Take note of funny tales you come across, whether it's a funny anecdote from your Grandma or something that happened at school. Besides keeping your audience engaged and entertained, funny stories will make them more likely to remember your story.

6. Take Time to Reflect

Reflection is a vital part of improving your storytelling skills. After hearing a funny story, take some time to reflect on it and think about what made it so funny and memorable. Consider the elements that made the story funny – the characters, dialogues, situations, etc. Try to break down the story into smaller sections and consider how each element contributes to the overall funny effect.

It's essential to consider why the story resonated with you and reflect on any changes that need to be made for it to have an even greater impact. This involves re-framing the narrative, introducing different characters, or changing the flow and pacing of the story.

Thinking about how laughter, humor, and wit play out in storytelling is vital. Reflection can help you identify funny stories overlooked or dismissed at first glance. It can allow you to look for jokes or funny moments that have yet to be noticed. Consider funny stories from different genres and explore how the humor works in each context.

Reflect on the lasting impact of funny stories and how they can affect you and others. Think about how funny stories can unite people, create a sense of connection, and inspire positive change. To have a lasting impact, funny stories must be carefully crafted and tailored to the listener. Reflection can help you identify what works and needs to be changed for your stories to make a lasting impression.

Unlock the Power of Listening to Become a Better Storyteller or Jokester!

Good listening skills will help you craft your own stories and ensure your tales are more engaging and entertaining for your audience.

Take the time to listen to others, be attentive and open-minded to different narrative styles, and look for areas where you can improve. Pay attention to the stories of others, both spoken and written. Listen closely to how they use language, the structure of their story, and any techniques they use to make it more captivating.

Taking in different points of view will help you expand your witty repertoire and become more creative with your own stories. Being an active listener can provide fresh insights and give you ideas for your jokes. Not every story you tell will be a success, but take note of the parts that worked and how they successfully engaged the audience.

By becoming a better listener, you'll be able to identify what works and doesn't and how to use this knowledge in your jokes. Good listening skills are essential for any jokester as they will help you create stories that captivate and engage listeners. So, hone your listening skills and become a better and wittier person.

By taking the time to listen, reflect, and document funny stories, you can become a master storyteller. Knowing how to craft compelling stories, utilize humor and wit effectively, and make your stories both memorable and impactful can help you become an engaging conversation starter or a captivating performer. Take advantage of the opportunity to hone your storytelling skills and keep track of funny stories for the next time you need a laugh.

Chapter 2: The Power of Laughing... At Yourself!

Have you ever noticed that some people could make others laugh just by being themselves? They have an effortless comedic charm that radiates from their very core and grabs everyone's attention. What is it that makes them so effortlessly funny? The secret lies in the power of self-deprecating humor – the art of laughing at oneself.

Do you want to be funny and make others laugh? That's awesome! But before you can do that, learn to laugh at yourself first. Laughing at yourself is powerful and can increase your confidence, charisma, and comedic abilities. It's surprising how a little self-deprecating humor can go a long way! Laughter is a superpower, and laughing at yourself will open up doors to a world of humor and self-acceptance.

By learning to laugh at yourself, you gain confidence and a better grasp of how to be funny.
https://www.pexels.com/photo/happy-woman-removing-face-mask-after-taking-bath-3852159/

Learning to laugh at yourself can break through social awkwardness, ease conversation tension, and create interesting jokes. In this chapter, we will explore the power of laughing at yourself and how it can help you become a funnier person whom others enjoy being around.

We'll discuss the different types of self-deprecating humor, how to use it effectively, and examples of people who have mastered this art. Knowing how to laugh at yourself is a valuable tool in anyone's arsenal and can unlock your inner comedian. So, let's get started!

What Does It Mean to Laugh at Yourself?

Laughing at yourself is an influential social skill. It's the ability to be comfortable in your skin and not take yourself too seriously. It's being able to laugh at yourself and not be afraid of making mistakes or coming across as foolish. When you make a mistake, laugh it off and then move on. It's okay to make mistakes; everyone does!

It's also about being open to humor and finding the funny side of things. It's about controlling your self-image and not letting others define you. When you laugh at yourself, it's a sign that you are comfortable in your skin and can accept your quirks and imperfections.

It implies understanding and accepting your faults, imperfections, and weaknesses. Rather than being ashamed of them or feeling guilty about them, you can use laughter as a form of self-acceptance. Doing this lets you let go of the barriers between you and others. You can relax, be yourself, and make jokes about your imperfections.

A Funny Self-Image

A strong sense of self is essential for comedy. Before making others laugh, you must be comfortable enough to poke fun at yourself without taking offense. As the saying goes: "You can't make others laugh at your expense if you don't laugh first." A healthy self-image is one of the keys to being funny.

The best way to build a healthy self-image is by learning to take jokes in your stride. If someone makes fun of you, don't take it personally. Instead of getting offended, learn to respond with a quip or joke of your own. Use humor as a defense mechanism instead of getting angry.

Another way to get comfortable with being funny is by coming up with jokes that make fun of your flaws or weaknesses. This is often a source of great hilarity, especially when done in good taste. For example, if you're not tech-savvy, you could joke about how you can't figure out the latest gadget. Or, if you're particularly clumsy, make a joke about tripping over yourself.

Finding Your Funny

The key to finding your unique brand of comedy is to pay attention to your natural reactions. You can learn to recognize the moments that make you laugh and draw humor out of those situations. Practice self-reflection and find out what kind of humor works best for you.

Learning to laugh at yourself will help you find humor in everyday scenarios. No matter how dire or frustrating a situation is, finding the funny in it can help reduce tension and make it more bearable.

Once you know what kind of humor works for you, it's time to develop your comedic voice. Think about the jokes you find funny or that make others laugh. Then, try to integrate those elements into your style. Also, practice telling jokes in front of a mirror or with friends. See what works and what doesn't, and use your feedback to improve your delivery.

The Value of Perspective

Once you've identified your delivery style, it's time to take a step back and gain perspective. Separating yourself from the moment can help you see the bigger picture, allowing you to add a layer of humor to your story. For example, if you find yourself in a situation that would normally make you feel embarrassed or angry, take a moment to step back and view it from a different perspective. You can look at the situation objectively and make a joke out of it.

Self-Deprecating Humor

Self-deprecating humor is comedy – where someone jokes about their attributes, flaws, or shortcomings. It can effectively make light of a situation, break down barriers and invite laughter. Self-deprecating humor ranges from simple jokes about clumsiness or lack of intelligence to more complex observations about a person's character flaws.

It can be a great way to form bonds with people because it permits those around you to laugh at your quirks or mistakes. It can make you seem more approachable and humbler, which makes people feel more comfortable around you.

At the same time, it is a delicate art and should be used with caution. If you go too far, it can make the people around you feel uncomfortable or even insulted. Always remember the context of the conversation and the kind of relationship you have with those around you.

The Art of Self-Deprecation

Self-deprecating humor is a great way to get people laughing while still maintaining your dignity. You don't have to be mean or harsh towards yourself; just find ways to make fun of yourself light-heartedly. It's a great way to show that you're secure in yourself and can poke fun at your shortcomings. The trick to being funny is to stay true to yourself. Take your unique qualities and quirks, and use them as comedic material.

Developing this art is a key skill to becoming a successful stand-up comedian. It takes courage and self-awareness to use your mistakes as comedic material, and it can go a long way in helping you build rapport with the audience. You can show your audience you're humble and in control by making light of awkward situations or mistakes.

Laughter is contagious, so when someone sees that you are comfortable enough to make jokes about yourself, they will be more likely to join in and have a good time.

The Benefits of Laughing at Yourself

Learning to laugh at yourself is a great way to manage your emotional and mental health. Studies show that laughing reduces stress hormones, improves mood, and can even help with physical ailments such as headaches and stomach aches. This kind of self-humor also helps you feel more confident and secure, as it is easier to take criticism if you can laugh at yourself.

Laughter as a Coping Mechanism

Humor can be used as a great form of self-care and psychological healing. It has been found to help reduce stress and anxiety, improve moods, increase empathy and understanding among people, lower blood pressure, reduce pain levels, and even boost the immune system. By learning to laugh at yourself, you can use laughter as a coping mechanism during difficult times and put things into perspective.

Brings Clarity

You can maintain your balance and perspective when you can laugh at yourself. Instead of being overly serious or too sensitive about a situation, laughing at oneself can often lighten the mood and make things easier to deal with. It allows us to be vulnerable and take risks without fear of feeling embarrassed or judged.

Making Others Laugh

Perhaps the biggest benefit of laughing at yourself is being able to laugh at other people's jokes - and even make your own! When we laugh at ourselves, we can appreciate other people's humor. Also, by learning to laugh at ourselves, we can create our own humor and stand-up comedy routines.

You create a safe environment where others don't feel self-conscious or judged when you laugh at yourself. Once they are comfortable, they can laugh, too, and that's when the real fun begins. Laughing at yourself can help break down social barriers by showing humility and self-awareness. It takes a special kind of person to laugh at themselves, and it can be an effective way to lighten up a conversation or bring people together.

Laughing at yourself is not just about having a good time; it's a way of developing self-awareness and understanding. When you can laugh at your mistakes, you become less afraid to take risks and make changes in your life. You'll also be less likely to take things too seriously or get offended when someone else playfully teases you.

By learning to laugh at yourself, you are taking responsibility for your emotions, which is integral to growing up and becoming a responsible adult. It's natural to want to be taken seriously by others, but being able to take yourself lightly gives you the emotional maturity needed to balance out an otherwise serious persona.

So, if you want to be funny, don't forget the essence of learning to laugh at yourself! Not only will it help you become a better comedian, but it will also help you live a healthier and happier life. Don't be afraid to let your goofy side show, and have fun with yourself; it might just be the best thing you ever do!

How to be Respectful When Making a Joke

When you're learning how to be funny, remember that certain topics or situations shouldn't be joked about. Making light of serious topics can make the joke-teller seem callous and insensitive and could easily offend the people around you.

That doesn't mean that you can't joke about topics such as sex, politics, or religion; just be sure to approach them with respect and tact.

When you're telling a joke about a sensitive topic, ensure it comes from a place of understanding and compassion. Try to relate the joke to your own experiences, or keep it light-hearted without being too flippant.

Humor can be a great way to show empathy and understanding, but thinking before speaking is essential. Everyone can interpret humor differently, so it's best to leave it out if you're unsure how a joke could be received.

Learning to be funny is about striking the right balance between being humorous and respectful. Keep this in mind as you practice your joke-telling skills. The more thoughtful and respectful you are when making jokes, the more likely people will appreciate them.

Be Mindful of Your Audience

When it comes to being funny, the people you're talking to are just as important as what you're saying. Depending on the situation, your jokes can land differently than you intended.

You'll want to be mindful of your topics and language in a professional setting. It's always best to err on the side of caution and not make jokes about anything that could be seen as offensive or inappropriate.

If you're in a casual setting with friends and family, you can usually feel more comfortable being yourself. Be sure to pay attention to how people respond. If someone looks uncomfortable or is not laughing, moving on to a different topic is best.

The key to being funny is understanding your audience and being mindful of the topics you joke about. By observing and listening, you'll be able to tell the kind of jokes that will make people smile and laugh!

The safest resort is to keep your jokes light-hearted and directed toward yourself rather than others. That way, you can laugh without hurting anyone else's feelings.

Remember, practice makes perfect when it comes to learning how to be funny. The more you tell jokes and get comfortable with yourself, the more confident you'll become.

Examples from Professionals

As you practice being funny, looking to professionals for inspiration is always helpful. Some of the funniest people in the world have mastered the art of making others laugh, so take a cue from them when crafting your jokes.

For instance, actor Tina Fey is known for her quick wit and clever observations about everyday life. She has an amazing ability to find humor in even the most mundane situations, and her jokes always seem to hit just the right note.

Comic book legend Stan Lee is another great example of a master joke teller. His witty one-liners often had people rolling in laughter, and his classic punchline delivery style was one of the reasons he was so successful.

Self-deprecating humor is Ricky Gervais' forte. He often jokes about his life and struggles, making him relatable to his audience.

Examples from Seasoned Actors

You don't have to be a professional stand-up comedian to be funny. Actors like Will Ferrell, Steve Carell, Emma Thompson, Seth Rogen, and Channing Tatum show that you can be naturally funny by playing with your personality and flaws. Take Will Ferrell, for example, who excels in roles that make fun of his own ridiculousness. His character Ron Burgundy from Anchorman, sees him stumble through the newsroom, taking everything in his stride. His characters often face humiliation, but Ferrell never takes himself too seriously, and this quality has made him beloved by fans everywhere.

Meanwhile, Steve Carell's characters in The Office and Despicable Me show off his knack for playing goofy yet lovable characters. He has a certain charm that can make even the most mundane situations hilarious.

Emma Thompson is another great example of an actor with a knack for comedy which plays on her wit and intelligence. She can deliver a cutting line with a deadpan expression, making her jokes all the more hilarious.

On the other hand, Seth Rogen and Channing Tatum make a great comedy duo, often relying on physical humor and improvisation to make audiences chuckle. Their antics in films like 21 Jump Street and This Is the End demonstrate how two people can play off each other to create an uproarious scene.

Take a few tips from these masterful funny people, and you'll be well on your way to bringing the laughs.

How to Be Funny While Keeping It Clean

Being funny takes work, but learning to observe and listen can hone your comedic timing and delivery. Ensure understanding of the source of humor by learning to appreciate irony and sarcasm. As you become more confident in your timing and delivery, you can introduce more subtle humor into your conversations and performances.

When it comes to being funny without offending, you must keep your humor clean and appropriate for the situation. Understand what kind of language and jokes are suitable for different audiences. If you're performing on stage, avoid profanity or overly sexual content. Know your audience and be mindful of potentially offensive topics.

Another way to be funny without offending is to observe the people and situations around you. Notice what's happening now, and you can find yourself with plenty of material for jokes. Get creative and use your imagination to devise clever puns, visual gags, and unexpected punchlines.

There's a lot to be said for self-deprecating humor. People usually relate to someone who can poke fun at themselves, making it a great way to break the ice. Remember that you can always make a joke about yourself without it not being warmhearted. For example, you can laugh at your misfortunes or insecurities, such as struggling to find a date or being clumsy. Share stories with amusing details; don't be afraid to laugh with your audience.

One anecdote is about my friend, who happened to be the most popular girl in school. She always made people laugh and enjoy her company, which made her very popular. On one occasion, she told a story about how she accidentally tripped at the mall and ended up in front of all these people. Everyone was laughing and having a great time until my friend stopped them abruptly and said, "But I got back up!" The whole room burst out into more laughter because it taught us such a crucial lesson. Even if you occasionally stumble along the way, always get back up!

By taking some cues from humorous people around you and learning to make light of situations, you'll be on your way to mastering the art of being funny. With practice, patience, and dedication, anyone can become funnier with time!

Another tip for mastering the art of being funny is not taking yourself too seriously. A certain level of humility comes with making jokes at your own expense, which can be nice for the people around you.

My other friend was a brilliant mathematics student who could solve complex equations in record time. He was also quite a jokester, often making light of his intelligence and ability to answer difficult questions. One day, he was working on a particularly difficult equation, and the professor asked him if he could solve it. His response? "I can try it, but if I do it wrong, don't blame me; my dad's a lawyer!" Everyone in the room erupted into laughter. Later, another student managed to answer the equation correctly.

This anecdote is a great example of how you can use self-deprecating humor as an effective way to make people laugh without being offensive. It shows humility and confidence and teaches us an essential lesson: even if you think you know something, don't be afraid to let someone else have their moment too! This type of humor requires subtly and timing, but it can make for some truly hilarious moments when used correctly.

Humor is all about finding fun in everyday life and not taking yourself too seriously. Once you learn to lighten up and share a few laughs with the people around you, it won't be long before you master the art of being funny. Allow yourself some moments to reflect or pause between jokes and witty remarks. This will make the funny moments stand out even more and give your audience time to appreciate and digest your jokes.

Though the journey may have its bumps along the way, with practice and dedication, anyone can become funnier in time. If you know how to observe people and situations, take cues from humorous people around you, understand irony and sarcasm, introduce subtle humor into conversations or performances, keep your humor clean and appropriate, and use self-deprecating jokes, you'll soon find that mastering the art of being funny isn't as hard as it seems. So, go ahead and give it a try. Make people laugh without taking yourself too seriously, and enjoy the journey along the way.

Chapter 3: How to Grab Anyone's Attention

In today's technological age, it may be tough to get someone's attention when everyone is staring at their phone, wearing headphones, or trying to juggle a dozen different tasks at once.

It isn't easy to get your audience's attention when so many other things compete for it. However, fortunately, several tactics are a sure approach to attracting your audience. You need to know how to develop a hook if you want your story, no matter what kind, to be read and shared.

In the same way that Christmas lights make a tree more attractive, a fascinating hook makes your content more appealing. While it isn't necessarily more vital than the content itself, it draws readers to your story.

Being able to grab anyone's attention requires a good hook.
https://www.pexels.com/photo/men-s-white-button-up-dress-shirt-708440/

The ability to craft a compelling hook that grabs your audience's attention is an invaluable skill we'll cover in this chapter.

What Is a Hook?

A hook (sometimes called a narrative hook) is the initial line or opening paragraph of a piece of writing intended to pique the reader's attention and keep them reading. A powerful hook will captivate readers by putting them in the heart of some dramatic event or raising interest in a fascinating character, uncommon scenario, or vital subject.

Storytellers use narrative hooks to draw in their listeners and keep them engaged. A narrative hook aims to help a storyteller successfully attract their audience's attention. In this context, "narrative" merely refers to a tale being told. In contrast, "hook" refers to the concept of an item grabbing something and pulling it along. Almost every tale starts with some hook, which helps to attract an audience's interest and entices them to spend more time in the story.

Expert Tip: *Don't write the hook until you've completed the whole piece. This will assist you in developing a relevant, innovative, and effective hook that underlines the content of your text. You'll have a more thorough grasp of the subject this way.*

What Is the Importance of a Good Hook?

No matter what you're writing, whether fiction (including short stories and novels) or non-fiction (including academic writing and narrative essays), a captivating opening is essential.

A hook line serves as an attention-getter and motivation for the audience to devote time and effort to your work. A good hook will keep the reader interested.

Different Types of Hooks (With Examples)

Below are different types of hooks with accompanying examples.

1. The Question Hook

An engaging question hook is a question that is relevant to the topic of your essay or report. The only way for someone to find out is to read what you have written.

People are naturally curious. Our natural curiosity is piqued whenever we have a question and are curious about the answer. When we don't know the answer, we always seek it out.

Writing your introduction as a question tells the reader they will get the answer if they read on.

A rhetorical question is another option. A rhetorical question is posed just for effect without expecting a response. The response could be clear or offered instantly by the questioner. Discreetly influence the sort of reaction you desire from your audience by asking them rhetorical questions. They can be coupled with figures of speech, puns, or double entendres for added dramatic or humorous impact.

You can begin your discussion by asking the following question to drive home your argument.

Examples

- *"Are you a happy saver, or do you like spending your money?"*

- *"Does the prospect of composing a blog post make your stomach turn?"*

- *"How much time does it take before you feel comfortable working on a brand-new project?"*

- *"How much of our beliefs and emotions are formed by our direct exposure to the world?"*

2. Provocative Statement

A confident declaration about your topic is a powerful statement. It's an effective strategy as the reader will be curious to know how you back up your claim regardless of whether or not they agree with you.

Examples

- *"It has long been believed that air (also known as argon) is the genesis of all life. In truth, the opposite is true. I've carved these lines to share how I learned to recognize the actual origin of life and, by extension, the mechanism by which all life will eventually come to an end."*

- *"It's funny that our current situations may be among the most romantic events we'll ever experience..."*

- *"Misconceptions abound when it comes to mental health. Many individuals assume mental health is genetically determined... Others feel it is merely a question of willpower... But the reality is somewhere in between."*

- *"Have you ever encountered a person who appears constantly invigorated and excited, as if they possess a hidden source of motivation? On the other hand, highly driven individuals do have a hidden motivation source. Some of them probably don't know what it is since it's so well hidden."*

- *"I don't know you, but I know this. You have access to the internet and sufficient free time to devote at least part of it to watching things on it. This may seem apparent, yet it informs me of two crucial things about you: For starters, you are in the upper half of humanity's wealth distribution... And two, you're probably battling a very contemporary human battle...: lethargy, boredom, self-doubt, and procrastination."*

3. Surprising Fact or Statistic

Facts and figures provide accurate information about a subject. They amaze the reader with proof right from the start of your piece. Creating rage or despair might be a great tactic since it promises release from those emotions towards the conclusion of your work.

You must incorporate information that is true, intriguing, and trustworthy. If you're going to share information, be sure that it comes from a reliable source.

Examples

- *"According to estimates, 99 percent of all species that have existed on earth are now extinct. "*

- *"Most pilots (43%-54%) confess to dozing off at the controls at least once. Almost one-third reported waking up to discover their co-pilot dozing."*

- *"There is a 35% increase in retweets for tweets with photos compared to those without."*

- *"80% of Soviet men born in 1923 died during WWII."*

- *"According to surveys, 28% of IT workers don't inform their loved ones about their profession for concerns about being burdened with requests to aid with computer problems."*

4. Personal Experience or Story

Audiences like stories that are well-written and memorable. This form of hook needs inspiration and imagination. It enables you to engage with your audience in a new and exciting manner.

Examples

- *"I recently got an email from "Be Yourself" anthology editor Joel Mwakasege, who offered some advice on "How a writer can bond with the audience. I feel obligated to apologize."*

- *"It was about two years ago. I was lounging on my couch, reading a Zat Rana article, when I was halted by an equation that described the beautiful personality and how to get it. The last line made me think about it. I began to wonder why I was hurting. When will it be enough, and why is it essential? What must I do? I sought a logical solution, and I found one today."*

- *"We were requested to estimate how long it would take to add a new feature to our program in one of my most recent projects. We got everything done, but it took three times as long to put into effect than had been anticipated. Unsatisfied with this outcome and looking for the cause of the difference between an estimate and actual labor, we discovered that we had overlooked the "training period" required by a developer participating in the project for the first time."*

- *"That wasn't the only reason our estimate was off. Still, I want to zero in on it and answer our project manager's question: "How long does it take to become comfortable with a new project?" I finally found the answer using the lessons I've learned through my successes and failures as a developer and recruiter over the last 14 years."*

- *"I, like many other people in the Angular community, have been watching the latest developments to learn what the next major version of the framework will offer us. Despite my research, I still feel like a complete amateur in computer programming. Despite my extensive background in Angular, I could not make sense of the information presented in those publications. So, I've taken it upon myself to produce a new article detailing the changes introduced by Angular 10 to make them more understandable."*

5. Quotation

Finding an appropriate motivational quotation to open your content is a great place to start. The reader can tell that you did some study for your work and will be more tempted to keep reading.

Choose a quote whose words are startling, strong, and unforgettable.

Examples

- *"Write as if no one is looking, because no one is."*

- *"Many of our dreams seem impossible at first, then unlikely, and then inevitable until we muster the courage to make them realistic."*

- *"The most potent weapon for changing the world is education."*

How to Grab Your Audience's Attention with an Excellent Hook

An excellent attention grabber may come to you with a spark of inspiration. It might be a challenge to your writing abilities sometimes to think of interesting ways to grab the reader's attention. If you're stuck for ideas for a decent hook, use this step-by-step strategy to create a terrific hook.

1. Startle the Reader with Your First Line

Using a surprising or exciting opening sentence may catch the reader off guard and entice them to read on.

A good example is the first sentence of the young adult book *"Not Our Summer." "Where does one even buy a brilliant green coffin like that?"*

This line does double duty by creating the scene and showing that the protagonist is as taken aback by the casket's unusual color as the reader is.

Create your own shocking opening sentence by using a character's confession, a stunning remark, or a query that stands out from the norm. Have some fun with it, and see what type of catchy opening line you can develop.

2. Begin with Action

This is the most common approach to immediately captivate a reader into a story. Not every exciting scene has a high-speed pursuit or an explosion. However, putting readers in the heart of a suspenseful moment will surely stimulate their attention.

Here is an excellent example from Ray Bradbury's "Fahrenheit 451":

"It was fun to burn.

Witnessing things devoured, blackened, and altered was a treat. The blood beat in his skull as he held the metal nozzle in his hands, this enormous serpent spewing its toxic kerosene into the globe. His fingers were the fingers of some fantastic conductor playing all the symphony of flaming and burning to take down the charred ashes of history."

Could you imagine a firefighter starting a fire instead of putting it out? This, my dear friend, is fascinating.

Other methods exist to create your own action-centered hook; it doesn't need to be a fire. The main character in your story may be on the run from someone. They may be getting into a fight. Alternatively, they may witness a crime. If necessary, you may use a flashback to apply this sort of hook. The choices are limitless.

3. Create an Emotional Bond

Don't waste your reader's time by starting them off in the middle of the action. Instead, try to get them invested in the story through an emotional scene. If you want your readers to care about what happens to a character in your story, you must give them a sense of that character's deeply emotional reaction.

Consider the following scenario from Walter Dean Myers' "Monster":

"Crying is most effective when no one can see your tears or when you hear someone being beaten and pleading for help in the dark. If you do this, people won't be able to hear you sneeze even if you're close. If someone overhears you sobbing, they'll start talking about it, and before you know it, you'll be beaten up after the lights go out."

This paragraph quickly makes the reader sympathize with the protagonist. We are undoubtedly worried for this person's well-being and would want to learn more about the circumstances.

Audiences may easily identify with your characters and care about what happens to them when you use emotions like shame, pity, anxiety, anticipation, surprise, and exhilaration.

4. Begin with a Life-Changing Experience

Another effective method is introducing – right off the bat – a defining event in the protagonist's life. Known as the *inciting event*, this is often the point in the story when the character is forced into a conflict. However, once they share this moment of transformation with the protagonist(s), readers will likely feel compelled to keep going.

Here's an excellent example from Franz Kafka's "Metamorphosis":

> *"When Gregor Samsa awoke from a dream, he transformed into a giant insect on his bed."*

A massive insect? If you're anything like me, you're dying to know what's happening around here.

Consider the inciting occurrence, and place it towards the beginning to pique the audience's interest in the character's journey, whether it be a literal one or one of symbolic significance.

5. Create Interest in the Characters

Every excellent story requires engaging characters, and it's possible to immediately hook your reader by referring to one of the characters' falsehoods, mysteries, or scandals. On the other hand, maybe your protagonist has a specific quality, like the main character of "Wonder" by R.J. Palacio:

> *"I realize I'm not your typical ten-year-old. Sure, I do commonplace stuff. I like eating ice cream. I go on a bike ride. I play baseball. I own an Xbox. Things like that make me average. I'm feeling unexceptional inside. But I know that regular kids do not make other regular kids flee screaming on playgrounds. I know normal kids don't attract unwanted attention everywhere they go."*

Our hearts go out to August after reading this first line. Still, we're curious as to why all the other kids in the neighborhood run away screaming whenever they encounter him. With this introduction, the story immediately inspires curiosity.

There are other techniques to generate interest in your characters in the same manner. To attract readers, emphasize your characters' unique qualities and what would make your readers want to learn more about them.

6. Begin from the Point of Confusion

Having your audience's mind boggled is a positive sign since it means they'll think critically about the story. People are more likely to feel invested in a story where the protagonist has an internal struggle early on, especially if that struggle causes them to question.

At the beginning of "That Weekend" (2021), Kara Thomas's book for young adults, the protagonist finds herself awake in the woods, hurt and bewildered. As a reader, you're desperate for an explanation of what happened and why she has no recollection of it.

Even if your protagonist doesn't have amnesia at the beginning of your story, you may still set the stage by having them enter a situation in which they have no idea what's happening. This will undoubtedly catch the audience's interest.

7. Use a Strong Tone to Captivate Your Audience

A writer's voice may be defined as their unique combination of diction, tone, perspective, and syntax, giving their writing a distinct feel and rhythm. It's what makes the protagonist in a first-person point-of-view story unique. It provides the third-person narrator with a distinctive voice. The best part of using a powerful voice is that it can immerse the reader in the story all on its own.

For example, consider Maverick's introductory scene in Angie Thomas' "Concrete Rose" (2021):

> "There are rules on the streets.
>
> They're not written down, and they're not in a book. It's natural things you've known since your mother allowed you out of the house. Similar to how you can breathe on your own without someone teaching you how."

Instantly, we get a sense of Maverick's personality, and we're intrigued to learn more about the topic to which he's hinting.

If you're starting as a writer, experiment with several voices until you discover one that fits your protagonist and the plot. Then, highlight that voice in the introduction to provide an engaging and memorable first impression.

8. Introduce Something Sinister

Another way to catch the audience is by immediately alluding to something strange or scary. In her 2011 book "Between Shades of Gray," Ruta Sepetys follows Lina, a young woman from Lithuania who is deported to a labor camp in Siberia during the Stalinist political repression of the mid-twentieth century. It begins with the following phrase:

"They picked me up in my nightgown."

This straightforward statement fuels our dread. What's more, we're curious about who may have abducted her. Why did they kidnap her? And what happened to her?

This is a good way to set the tone for a narrative with a dark or foreboding theme. Give readers knowledge that both frightens them and draws them into the tale.

9. Try to Avoid Using Descriptive Language

Knowing what to omit is critical when developing a hook that grabs your audience's attention. Unless doing so would disclose something new or exciting about the character, it is advisable to avoid beginning with a description of everyday acts like waking up, having breakfast, or getting dressed. Remember that you have a few pages to entice your reader. Descriptions, although wonderful, aren't always intriguing. Instead, keep to in-the-moment action, conversation, and narrative, particularly in the first few pages.

10. Keep Your Audience's Attention Once You've Got It

A brilliant hook will capture your audience's interest, but it is your duty *to keep it.* Too many unresolved questions may be frustrating, but resolving every question immediately offers readers little incentive to continue reading. This attention-holding strategy requires a delicate balance, but the ideal way to accomplish it is by addressing some of the issues raised by your hook while adding new ones to keep the reader guessing.

Referring back to Kara Thomas's "That Weekend," our heroine wakes up lost in the woods but is eventually found by a woman and her dog, who explain their whereabouts. She recalls that it is prom day and spent it in a friend's cabin, but neither the friend nor her lover can be located. The author creates an even more intriguing puzzle for the protagonist and the reader.

A hook's only purpose is to grab the audience's interest immediately. We want our readers to feel immersed in our story and ready to stay to the end, right? Luckily, there are many options available. Experiment with different hooks until you find one that complements the tale you want to convey.

All you have to do is remember the tips above and use the examples provided as guides, and you'll have a great beginning to your own story.

Chapter 4: The Three Cs: How to Be Chill, Comfortable, and Confident When Telling a Joke

Want to be funny and charming without putting in too much effort? It's possible, and having a great sense of humor can boost your charisma and likability. However, many people, like the author of "The Art of Witty Banter," Patric King, make the mistake of trying to imitate others' comedic styles and techniques. Patric admired David Letterman and tried to emulate his presenting skills and confidence, but it didn't go well. The key is to master techniques and make them your own. This chapter will show you how to appear confident, comfortable, and relaxed while telling jokes and holding an audience's attention.

Confidence is key to having an appealing sense of humor.
https://www.pexels.com/photo/two-women-smiling-908602/

Being funny and charismatic often go hand in hand. To make people laugh and command attention, you must be comfortable in your skin and at ease in any situation. However, being chill and confident when telling jokes or being humorous doesn't come naturally to everyone, but it is a skill that can be developed with practice and training.

In this chapter, we'll explore the three Cs of comedy: chill, comfort, and confidence, and how mastering them can help you be more successful at making people laugh.

Being chill means staying cool, calm, and collected in difficult or stressful situations. It involves being relaxed, easygoing, and not letting things get to you. In telling jokes, being chill means not getting too worked up or anxious about whether or not your joke will land. It means being confident about making people laugh and not getting too caught up in the outcome.

To be comfortable telling a joke, you need to be at ease, feel confident in your delivery, and not be self-conscious or nervous. Being comfortable also means being familiar with your material and having a good sense of timing.

Confidence is crucial when it comes to telling a joke. You may be uncertain or hesitant without confidence, which can ruin the punchline. Confidence also comes from being well-prepared and knowing your material. Believing in your ability to make people laugh and not doubt yourself is important.

How to Be Chill

Being chill means staying cool, calm, and collected in difficult or stressful situations. It involves being relaxed, easygoing, and not letting things get to you. Here are some tips for how to be chill:

1. Practice Mindfulness

One of the key aspects of being chill is being present in the moment and not letting your mind wander to worries about the past or future. Mindfulness involves paying attention to your thoughts and feelings in a non-judgmental way and can help you stay centered and grounded. You can practice mindfulness by focusing on your breath, paying attention to your senses, or doing a mindful activity like coloring or knitting.

2. Take Care of Your Physical and Emotional Health

Being chill requires physical and emotional resilience. Ensure you get enough sleep, eat healthily, and exercise regularly to keep your body and mind in good shape. Take breaks when needed, and make time for activities that nourish your soul, like hobbies, socializing, or self-care.

3. Learn to Manage Stress

Stress is a natural part of life, and learning how to manage it is part of being chill. You can try many different stress management techniques, like exercise, deep breathing, journaling, or talking to someone about your feelings. Experiment with different approaches and find what works best for you.

4. Accept That You Can't Control Everything

One of the main sources of stress is the desire to control every aspect of our lives. But the reality is that there are many things we can't control, and trying to do so is often futile leading to frustration. Instead of trying to control everything, focus on what you can control and let go of the rest. This can help you feel more relaxed and accepting of whatever comes your way.

5. Set Boundaries

Another way to be chill is to set boundaries for yourself and others. This means knowing your limits and being clear about what you are and are not willing to do or accept. Setting boundaries can help you feel more in control of your life and reduce the stress you experience.

6. Practice Gratitude

Focusing on what you are thankful for can also be a big help. Take a few minutes each day to think about what you are grateful for, and start a gratitude journal. This will help you shift your perspective and focus on the good things in your life.

7. Find Ways to Relax

Hobbies or doing something you enjoy always helps you relax and unwind. This could be anything from meditation and yoga to reading or listening to music. Set aside some daily time for relaxation, and try to do at least one thing each week that brings you joy and helps you relax.

8. Don't Take Things Too Seriously

It's natural to get caught up in the drama and stress of everyday life, but it's fruitless to take things too seriously. Try to find humor in situations; don't be afraid to laugh at yourself. This can help you stay more chill and not get too worked up over things that don't matter in the long run.

9. Learn to Say No

It's okay to prioritize your own needs and well-being. Saying no can be difficult, especially if you tend to be a people-pleaser. But learning to set limits and say no to things that don't align with your values or goals can help you feel more in control and reduce stress.

10. Practice Patience

Being chill often requires patience and flexibility, especially when things don't go according to plan. Instead of getting frustrated or upset, take a step back and accept that sometimes things don't go as planned.

11. Practice Forgiveness

Holding grudges and being angry or resentful can affect your mental and emotional well-being. Practice forgiveness, not just for the benefit of others, but for your own peace of mind. This doesn't mean that you have to forget what happened or continue to be in a relationship with someone who has wronged you, but it does mean letting go of negative emotions and moving on.

12. Don't Sweat the Small Stuff

It's easy to get caught up in the little things that go wrong in life, but remember that most are small and inconsequential in the greater scheme of things. Don't let them get to you and ruin your day. Practice letting goes of perfectionism and focusing on the bigger picture.

13. Practice Good Communication

Good communication is important in any relationship and can help you feel more connected and understood. This means being honest and open with others and being willing to listen to their perspectives. It also means setting clear boundaries and being assertive when you need to be.

14. Don't Compare Yourself to Others

Comparison is often the thief of joy, leading to feelings of inadequacy and stress. Instead of comparing yourself to others, focus on your own progress and accomplishments. Remember that everyone has their journey, and being on your own path is okay.

15. Be Kind to Yourself

Be gentle with yourself and practice self-compassion. This means understanding and supporting yourself, especially when you make mistakes or face challenges. Remember that everyone has off days, and it's okay not to be perfect.

Being chill is not about being passive or ignoring your feelings but rather about finding balance and staying centered in the midst of life's ups and downs. It takes practice and patience, but with time and effort, you can learn to be more chill and enjoy a more peaceful and fulfilling life.

How to Do All the Three Cs

Now that you are familiar with the three Cs, it's time to build your understanding and skills. Remember that becoming proficient in using humor will take time and practice, even with this practical guide. However, with dedication and the following key tips, you can confidently and comfortably inject humor into your interactions.

1. Observe Your Surroundings and Read the Room

To be funny, paying attention to the atmosphere and the people around you is important. Notice the energy in the room and the type of jokes that are getting a response. It's also helpful to ask open-ended questions to get to know your audience better and find relatable topics. However, avoid making all the jokes about yourself, and respect the room's mood.

If the atmosphere is tense, it's best not to try to be funny. Instead, try to match the energy of the room. Remember that you can't control how others react to your jokes, so focus on being your best self. Don't let negative energy from the room affect you; try to steer it in a positive direction instead. When you're speaking to an audience, it's important to remain calm and collected. This will help you stay in control of the situation and not be thrown off by reactions or worries about what others think of you. Focus on what makes you happy and what you want.

2. Vibe Evenly with the Space You Are In

When telling jokes, consider the mood of your space. If you're in a serious meeting, it's probably inappropriate to start cracking jokes. On the other hand, if you're at a party with friends, you can loosen up a bit. It's necessary to understand the expectations of the space and whether or not the mood is receptive to humor. If the mood is tense, think carefully about whether or not your joke will be well-received. Remember that you can only control your own behavior. If you start getting too energetic, try to stay calm and collected. Anticipate how your words and actions may affect the room, and be prepared to adjust your behavior accordingly. If the room gets too loud or crazy, it may be time to pull back.

3. Remember That You Can Only Control Yourself

Remember, you cannot control others or external circumstances, only yourself. This may seem obvious, but it is an important lesson to remember. Pay attention to how you present yourself to others and the energy you exude. If you feel nervous, take some deep breaths, and try to relax rather than resist the feeling. Remember that your audience wants you to succeed and make them laugh, so permit yourself to be funny and trust that it will come naturally with effort.

4. Know That Less Is More

When telling a joke, using fewer words for maximum impact is better than adding unnecessary flourishes. This can help you appear more confident and ensure your joke is not lost among unnecessary details. Remember that while having good jokes is important, *the way you present them* is just as crucial. So, don't worry too much about the quality of your material. Just focus on being relaxed, confident, and comfortable.

5. Think of Yourself as Cool

To be confident and deliver a good joke, you must believe in your coolness and uniqueness. This means letting go of any negative self-talk or comparison and finding a comfortable place to be yourself without fear of judgment. To get there, try practicing visualization techniques or writing daily affirmations like "I am funny!" Remember that your main goal when telling a joke is to make the audience feel comfortable. This can be achieved by having a relaxed mentality and demeanor.

6. Focus on Wants, Not Shoulds

It's easy to get caught up in what we "should" do or think to please others, but this mentality can be difficult to maintain. This means not trying too hard or putting yourself in situations in which you don't feel comfortable. Instead, focus on what you truly want and be true to yourself when presenting your jokes. Remember, the more relaxed and confident you are, the more your audience will enjoy your jokes. So let go of the pressure and have fun!

7. Practice Saying No

Setting boundaries can be challenging, especially regarding conversations and sharing stories. That's why it's important to practice saying no. This helps you feel more confident and comfortable with yourself and gives you the strength to assert yourself. You can practice saying no by setting limits for yourself, such as how many jokes you will tell or how much time you will spend talking with someone. By understanding your boundaries, you can become a more effective communicator and better at reading other people's reactions.

Saying no also demonstrates that you are in control of your storytelling and trust your instincts about what works best for you. It also helps to reduce feelings of being overwhelmed or uncomfortable with what is expected of you in any situation. Knowing that you can say no gives you the power to take charge, stay calm, and be confident.

8. Be Proactive, Not Reactive

Stay proactive rather than reactive to exude confidence and maintain your chill. Avoid letting the emotions of the crowd overwhelm you. If something doesn't go as expected, handle it gracefully, and don't let it shake your cool. Instead, focus on what you can do to get back on track. Pay attention to your reactions and the reactions of others, and make decisions accordingly. People will respond positively to your story or joke when you have the right attitude and energy. By practicing proactivity and remaining mindful, being chill, comfortable, and confident can become second nature.

Examples of Chill, Confident and Comfortable Jokes and Why They Fit the 3 Cs

Here are a few examples of chill, confident, and comfortable jokes and why they fit the three Cs:

- *"Why was the mathematics book depressed? Because it has many problems."* This joke is chill because it is light. It doesn't try too hard to be funny and doesn't rely on shock value. It is confident because it is delivered in a matter-of-fact way, without hesitation or uncertainty. And it is comfortable because it is relatable and not offensive or controversial.

- *"Why can't the bicycle stand on its own? Due to the fact that it is two-tired."* This joke is chill because it is straightforward. It is confident because it is delivered with a clear and confident delivery. And it is comfortable because it is not likely to offend anyone and can be enjoyed by a wide audience.

- *"I just got a new job at the butter factory. I'm spreading myself thin."* This joke is chill because it is self-deprecating and doesn't take itself too seriously. It is confident because it is delivered with a calm and assured demeanor. And it is comfortable because it is relatable and not offensive.

- *"What caused the tomato to become red? It noticed the condiment."* This joke is comfortable because it is self-deprecating and doesn't take itself too seriously. It also suggests that the speaker is open to learning and growth.

- *"Why was the computer cold? It left its Windows open."* This joke is chill because it is a simple play on words and doesn't rely on shock value or edginess.

- *"I'm not arguing; I'm just explaining why I'm right."* This joke is confident because it is self-assured and doesn't shy away from stating a strong opinion.

- *"I'm not arguing; I'm just trying to converse with a higher IQ than my own."* This joke is comfortable because it is self-deprecating and doesn't take itself too seriously. It also suggests that the speaker is open to learning and growth.

Overall, the key to telling a chill, confident, and comfortable joke is to keep it light, relatable, and inoffensive and to deliver it in a relaxed and assured manner.

Tips and Tricks to Deliver the Best Jokes

Know your audience: Make sure your jokes are appropriate for the people you are telling them to. Different groups will find different things funny, so it's important to consider to whom you are telling the joke. Here are some tips and tricks for delivering the best jokes:

Timing is key: The delivery of a joke is just as important as the joke itself. Pay attention to your pacing and pause at the right moments to build up to the punchline.

Confidence is key: If you don't believe in your joke, chances are your audience won't either. Deliver your jokes with confidence and conviction.

Facial expressions and body language can help sell the joke and add to the overall comedic effect.

Practice, practice, practice: The more you tell a joke, the more comfortable you will become with it. This will help you deliver it with confidence and timing.

Don't be afraid to tailor the joke: If you are telling a joke you heard from someone else and it's not landing with your audience, don't be scared to change it up and make it your own.

Don't take yourself too seriously: The best comedians can laugh at themselves and their material. Don't be afraid to poke fun at yourself and your jokes.

Most importantly, have fun! If you have a good time telling the joke, chances are your audience will too.

To be funny, be comfortable with yourself, and exude confidence. Feeling comfortable in your skin means matching the energy of your surroundings and remembering that you can only control yourself. Observing your surroundings and reacting appropriately can help you find your "chill" and understand the energy of the room. Remember that *less is often more* when it comes to humor. Instead of focusing on what you think you should do, consider what you want to do and be proactive. Practice is key when it comes to telling jokes, and with the right practice, you can go from being an amateur to a highly funny person. With intention and effort, you will see results quickly. Go out and start spreading smiles!

Chapter 5: The Importance of Timing and Tone

Timing and tone are essential elements when it comes to delivering a funny, humorous joke or sketch. Unfortunately, getting the timing and tone just right can be difficult, especially for novice comedians. The good news is that this chapter provides a comprehensive insight into mastering the importance of timing and tone to unleash the full potential of your humor. You will learn the basics of how to control your voice, gestures, and volume to ensure that your jokes land with audiences. With each practice you undertake, you will understand how to make use of pauses, repetition, and speed to set up laughs from your audience. So, if you have been wondering how to time and tone comedic lines for maximum impact, this chapter has all the answers for you.

When it comes to comedy, your timing and tone could make all the difference.
https://www.pexels.com/photo/photo-of-two-laughing-women-walking-past-graffiti-wall-2346701/

Why Is Timing Important in Comedy?

1. Timing Sets Up the Joke

Knowing how to time comedy is key to being an entertaining storyteller. Comedians and actors often need to master timing when delivering their jokes or lines so that they will have the desired effect on the audience. If a joke or line is delivered too soon, it can completely lose its impact. On the other hand, if it's delivered too late, then the audience can feel confused or bored. Good timing sets up a joke so that it becomes funny or revealing at the right moment. For example, if a comedian was to ask, "Why did the chicken cross the road?" he/she would wait for the audience to expect a punchline before announcing, "To get to the other side!" This type of timing creates anticipation from the audience, leading to rolling laughter and applause when done correctly. Likewise, some lines within plays require perfect timing for maximum effect. An actor's slight change of delivery can cause the entire dynamic between two characters to be suddenly thrown off balance for humorous results. Timing is critical in comedy because it's what helps make jokes hilarious and captivating for audiences everywhere.

2. Timing Allows for Build Up

Timing also helps to build up tension in a joke, making it funnier when the punchline is delivered. Suppose a comedian moves too quickly from setup to punchline. In that case, the joke lacks any sort of buildup and fails to create anticipation for the payoff. When done correctly, timing can make a joke much more effective by setting up the proper tension before the punchline. A great example of this happened in the 1992 movie "My Cousin Vinny," when Marisa Tomei's character Mona Lisa Vito sets up a crucial joke by saying, "I objected to a series of questions" before waiting for a beat, letting everyone expect the punchline. When Joe Pesci's character Vincent Gambini delivers the punchline, "You objected to the series? Was it a good show?", it has double the impact due to Tomei's excellent timing. Similarly, famous stand-up comedians such as Eddie Murphy and Chris Rock have mastered timing within their monologues, knowing that pausing at just the right moment can make an audience laugh harder. It is clear that when it comes to comedy, timing really is everything.

3. Timing Creates Variety

Good timing also breaks up the monotony in comedy, allowing for moments of surprise and uniqueness that can keep an audience engaged. If a joke is delivered with perfect timing, it has the potential to break up the rhythm of a set and surprise an audience in the best way possible. An example of great timing can be seen in movies such as "The Hangover," where each character delivers a punchline right after another, often without any prompt or sound effects, just with their expressions and movements. In addition, stand-up comedians can use timing to create a variety of comedic moments within monologues. This could include pauses for audience laughter or to create a jarring contrast between unrelated topics.

4. Timing Can Help with Improvisation

Good timing also helps with improvisational comedy, enabling comedians to think on their feet and react quickly to any situation. Strong timing can help comedians come up with witty punchlines and responses at the moment, allowing them to make an audience laugh with their quick thinking and comedic timing. It takes a keen sense of timing to be able to deliver the right punchline or response at the right moment, which can make all the difference between a successful comedic performance and one that falls flat. To be an effective improviser, learn how to use timing as an improvisational tool. This could involve taking a pause before delivering your answer or responding quickly with a witty quip, whichever works at the moment. Luckily, there are many examples of great comedic timing in movies and from famous stand-up comics that you can use as inspiration. Watching scenes with hilarious movie quotes, like "Good morning, Vietnam!" or taking note of timeless monologues by comedians such as Eddie Murphy, are great for honing your comedic timing and will help you tremendously.

5. Timing Can Enhance Unexpectedness

Good comedic timing also helps enhance the unexpectedness of a joke, as it permits a comedian to set up a joke in one way but then deliver it in another. This unexpected twist can make a joke even funnier, as it empowers anyone to surprise an audience with their timing and delivery. A joke can get an even greater reaction than expected with good comedic timing. However, unexpectedness does not have to come in the form of a punchline. Pausing for a beat at the right moment can create suspense, drawing the audience into the story and heightening anticipation before delivering a comedic reveal. For example, in "Get Smart," when Agent Maxwell Smart disguises himself as a painting that comes alive after Buck Henry pauses dramatically. Another great example of comedic timing is John Cleese's masterpiece jump cut, "Ministry of Silly Walks," which combines perfectly timed facial expressions and body movements to make audiences howl with laughter.

Why Is Tone Important in Storytelling?

The tone of a story or comedic performance is an essential component of successful storytelling. It provides the audience with an emotional cue that helps them to connect with the material, and it can be used by comedians to great effect when crafting their performances. Tone is also vital in creating a sense of humor and providing a subtle layer of meaning or message within the work.

At its most basic level, tone is how we interpret emotions expressed through words and vocal inflection. This helps give a character's dialogue life and allows us to relate more easily to their experiences. Whether we're reading a novel, watching a movie, or listening to stand-up comedy, we rely on the emotion behind each line to help tell the story.

A great example of this can be found in the HBO show, "Curb Your Enthusiasm." Larry David's signature dry and sarcastic delivery provides a unique tone to each scene that evokes both humor and sometimes even sympathy from the audience. Even when Larry is portrayed as an antihero or bad person, his delivery creates a sense of relatability and makes us laugh despite ourselves.

In comedy, tone is used to maximize the impact of jokes by providing context or adding an extra layer of irony or sarcasm. For example, consider the classic stand-up routine of legendary comedian Rodney Dangerfield. He often uses exaggerated vocal inflection and body language to emphasize his trademark phrase: "I don't get no respect!" This delivery helps to add emphasis and humor to his jokes and provides a broader message about the human condition.

Tone is also essential in conveying emotional depth to characters within a story. Consider the critically acclaimed Pixar movie "Up!" The varying tones of voice used by Ed Asner as Carl Frederickson tell us just as much about his character's journey and emotions as any dialogue ever could. We feel the sadness of his lost love, joy at each new adventure, and acceptance when he finds peace with his situation.

In conclusion, tone plays a key role in storytelling and comedy by helping audiences connect emotionally with the material. It provides subtle layers of meaning that can help bring out humor and emotion in performance and can be used to create an atmosphere that audiences will remember long after the show. Knowing how to use tone effectively is essential for any great storyteller or comedian.

How to Get Better at Timing and Tone

1. Learn to Read the Room

One of the keys to success is being able to read the room. Understanding the context of your audience's reaction will give you clarity on how far you should push a joke and how you need to adjust your humor accordingly. It's significant to be aware of where your jokes land and how receptive or resistant the audience is to certain topics or humor types. Doing this can help guide your content so that it resonates with them and even leave them with a good impression of the show they just watched.

2. Play with Different Tones and Inflections When Delivering a Joke

Learning to deliver a joke with perfect timing and tone requires some practice. One great way to get better at it is to play with different inflections when delivering a joke. A slight variation in your voice can make all the difference in how a joke lands. This could include speaking louder or softer, slowing down or speeding up, adding pauses between words, or even stretching out syllables. Even if it doesn't always result in hysterical laughter, varying your tone of telling a joke will provide an extra bit of emphasis and give you more control over the audience's reaction to it. Additionally, vary the volume of your delivery based on what type of audience you are in front of. In large audiences, you should project your voice more than if you were in a smaller set of people. Then experiment with pitch, pacing, and pauses for added comedic effect.

3. Practice, Practice, Practice!

Whether you're writing jokes for stand-up comedy or trying to become more comfortable making puns in conversation, the best way to get better at timing and tone is through repetition and feedback from others. Getting better at timing and tone when being humorous or doing comedy requires more than just a funny concept. Practicing delivery is key. Different comedic styles require different tones of voice, timing, and pace, and the only way to learn when to say what with the right inflection is through practice and patience. Work on your jokes in front of a mirror or film yourself telling jokes. Listen back critically, or get feedback from others, to develop an ear for where you could add emphasis or tell it faster for greater impact. The more you practice, the more natural your delivery will become, and the better your audience will receive your jokes. Just remember that practice makes perfect.

4. Watch Sitcoms, TV Series, and Stand-up Sets

Comedy can be a powerful tool to take any conversation, presentation, or speech up a notch. Even while it might seem like certain people have a natural gift for humorous timing and tone, everyone can improve with the correct training and direction. Watching a variety of comedy sketches, stand-up performances, sitcoms, films, and other forms of comedy is one great way for both aspiring comedians and regular people alike to sharpen their comedic skills. This type of "watching" practice allows you to see how professional comedians structure their jokes and perform with different tones of voice or emphasis on words or expressions. It also helps with recognizing timing opportunities within conversations and everyday situations. Watching and analyzing the comedic timing and delivery used by experienced comedians can give you an idea of how to craft your own jokes in terms of timing and delivery. The key is to pay attention to specific techniques they use in various settings and do your best to use them yourself in conversations, eventually becoming more skilled at timing overall.

Watching comedians at work will help you pick up on cues, tone, and timing for better jokes.
https://www.pexels.com/photo/group-of-people-watching-gray-laptop-computer-1595387/

5. Record Yourself

Timing and tone are critical when humorously engaging an audience. One of the best ways to improve timing and delivery is to record yourself performing your comedy material. This simple yet powerful strategy creates an opportunity to listen back, assess, and refine your comedic approach as you review how it sounds to others. You can practice honing your sense of timing and tone during this process and gain a stronger understanding of your performance style, leading to more consistent delivery. Recording yourself is a definite win-win for anyone who wants to heighten their comedic ability! Taking the time to record your jokes and plays can help you identify any timing issues or awkward pauses, allowing you to adjust them before they become obvious while performing.

6. Take Note of Successful Comedians

Watch experienced comics on television or in person, paying attention to how they deliver their lines and use tone and inflection to get a laugh from their audience. Notice the timing of their jokes and try to replicate their techniques when making your own comedic material. It is also useful to watch a variety of stand-up comedians to get an idea of the range of humor and tones that can be used for comedic effects. Try to identify different comedic styles, such as physical, observational, or self-deprecating humor, and then see how each comedian uses pauses to get their point across. By studying successful jokes, you can figure out which techniques work best for you and your audience. Notice what did and didn't work for each comedian so you can learn from their successes and mistakes. This will help you develop your own unique style. When constructing jokes, use the same techniques that successful comedians use to increase the odds that your material will be well received. Try out the timing of each joke before you perform it in front of an audience so that you know when to pause for emphasis and when to ramp up the intensity. Be sure to incorporate appropriate facial expressions and body language into your delivery to draw out the humor of any joke. By studying successful comedians and imitating their techniques, you can get better at timing and tone when being humorous or doing comedy.

7. Know When to Take a Break

Suppose you're feeling overwhelmed by trying too hard to be funny or telling too many jokes at once. In that case, it can help to pause for a moment and allow the audience some time for reflection before continuing with your routine. Not only will this give the audience time to reflect, but it can also help you get better at timing and delivery. Knowing when to take a break when being humorous or doing comedy is an invaluable skill and one that takes practice to perfect. Jokes falling flat with audiences can often be salvaged by taking a beat and waiting for the audience to stop laughing before continuing. Pausing can also help to create tension in the room, making the next joke more impactful and greater appreciated. Keeping track of timing can be difficult at first, but like anything else, it requires practice. It's significant to pay attention to how laughter or silence changes the flow of a joke or comedy routine and use it as a gauge when deciding how dynamic your timing should be throughout each performance. With enough trial and error, you'll soon find yourself mastering the art of funny, both in terms of content and timing.

8. Introduce Humor Gradually

Humor is a tricky beast. If you try too hard or move too quickly, it can fall flat and make you look awkward. Don't rush into a joke or try to be too funny too quickly. Start by making more general observations, which will allow the audience time to become comfortable with your style of comedy before delving deeper into more humorous topics. It's best to introduce humor gradually, build up the tension and wait for the right moment. Use your sense of timing to decide when this moment comes, allowing your listener to initially warm up to your joke without feeling overwhelmed by it. When done correctly, you can use humor as an effective way to connect with someone and get them engaged in conversation. With enough practice, you'll get better at recognizing when and how to use humor appropriately, so don't be afraid to experiment!

9. Have Fun

For normal people looking to get better at timing and tone when doing comedy, remember that the enjoyment of comedy is that it is supposed to be shared. Not only should the audience have fun, but the person telling jokes or doing comedy should also find joy in it. When having fun, it's easier to take risks by trying new things and helping develop comedic timing and tone. Doing practice delivery runs can help one determine the best way to structure a joke so that everything comes together perfectly. Comedy isn't about perfection. It's about having fun and appreciating an enjoyable experience with others. This will naturally lead to better timing and delivery of your jokes as you become more confident in your comedic abilities.

10. Take Cues from Your Audience

A great way to improve timing and tone when being humorous or doing comedy is to take cues from your audience and environment. Being aware of body language, facial expressions, and the room's atmosphere will help you understand how far your joke should go. Pay attention to the cues that people give off, whether they're laughing, applauding more slowly than usual, or just staring blankly in bewilderment. Notice what kind of jokes get applause or tumble flat to find out what works best for them. It can be helpful to practice before actually performing, but using real-time audience feedback will greatly help your comedic timing and style.

11. Be Humble and Don't Take Yourself too Seriously

Humor and comedy are popular forms of entertainment and can be a great way to engage people, connect with them on a different level, and bring joy to their lives. But remember that if you want to execute it correctly and ensure you get the timing and tone just right, then it is key to be humble and not take yourself too seriously. By staying humble and not taking yourself too seriously, you will lower your guard and give yourself more freedom to truly express creativity in your comedic act. Try not to judge yourself too harshly for any mistakes or projects that either fail or under-perform because those experiences will help you learn from them, grow from them, and develop more wit in your humor so that the next time you do it, you can find success with perfect timing and tone.

12. Experiment with Different Delivery Styles

Experiment with different delivery styles to become more proficient in humor and comedy. Humor is subjective, so what may work for one person would not be as successful for a different audience. Include pauses and increasing or decreasing voice inflection when delivering punchlines while experimenting. It's also beneficial to practice in front of friends or family first so they can give you feedback on how the jokes are landing before doing a big performance. Spontaneity helps, too. Those who naturally react quickly and think outside the box often produce the most memorable comedic moments. Taking the time to understand different scenarios among audiences helps to have a better-timed reaction that evokes laughter from all involved.

13. Take Risks

If you're looking to become a better comedian or hone your comedic timing, taking risks is the way to get there. Trying new material and pushing the boundaries can help you find the right tone and determine what's funny, so don't be shy. Not every joke will work, and that's okay. Use what you've learned from those fails, adjust your routine as needed, and keep practicing until it's refined for maximum hilarity. Taking risks can open up new avenues in humor, so never shy away from trying something new.

14. Learn Improvisation

In addition to watching a comedy or practicing improvisation, reading articles written by professionals on comedy writing can give you insight into how humor works in terms of scripting your jokes as well as their delivery. Knowing the types of jokes that work best for live audiences or recorded media can help you understand comedic timing better. Additionally, reading books on stand-up comedy, such as "The Comedy Bible" by Judy Carter, can provide invaluable advice from experienced stand-up comedians on crafting punchlines and developing memorable characters for your act.

15. Join a Workshop

Humor can be a difficult talent to nurture, but with the help of stand-up comedy workshops or classes, everyday people can learn how to hone timing and tone when it comes to delivering their jokes. Participants of these courses are trained to understand their audience before beginning a set, creating material based on personal experiences, and learning about types of funny styles that work for certain situations. Moreover, not only does studying stand-up help individuals better appreciate the comedic craft, but it also helps build their confidence in expressing themselves in a humorous way while keeping an audience engaged. With practice and dedication to one's craft, anyone can learn how to become a top-notch comedian.

Chapter 6: Body Language Hacks for Funny Folks

The topic of body language is vast and often difficult to comprehend. Many people wonder how to use body language for humor and storytelling. Thankfully, this chapter will provide readers with Body Language Hacks for Funny Folks so that everyone can access easy-to-follow techniques for using body language to capture an audience's attention. Through specific tips for hands, posture, facial expressions, and eye contact, readers will gain useful insight into how to utilize their physicality to get the audience laughing. It is all about confidence. Execute these hacks correctly, and no one will doubt the creativity or comedic genius of the person performing them!

Eye Responses

Using your eyes to add expression is one of the most crucial elements in comedic storytelling. A simple widening of eyes or raising of brows can emphasize key points and create humorous moments. In movies, comedians, and TV series, different types of eye expressions have been used to great effect to bring out audiences' laughs.

For example, looking up with surprise at something unexpected conveys a sense of disbelief, which can be enhanced by a wide-eyed expression that emphasizes your shock. This can be used to humorous effect when the speaker is not expecting a certain outcome or when something unexpected occurs, creating an amusing moment that elicits laughter from the audience.

Using your eyes and eyebrows in a number of ways can help express humor.
https://www.pexels.com/photo/woman-in-blue-crew-neck-shirt-3766212/

In particular, humorous stories benefit from eye responses that draw attention to the humor. For example, comedians often use exaggerated eye expressions, such as rolling or widening in surprise, when they perform on stage. This helps illustrate the joke rather than simply relying on words alone. Similarly, movie actors use subtle yet expressive eye movements to indicate when something funny is happening or about to occur.

Looking to one side with raised eyebrows and lowered eyes can express confusion and disbelief in a funny way. This expression is often used by comedians who are trying to make light of a situation for comedic effect. The exaggerated eye movements create an absurdly comical visual that will draw laughs from audiences. Another type of eye response that can generate humor is squinting or narrowing one's eyes as if suspicious or angry at something. Squinting gives off a menacing feeling, but it can also be used in comedic ways, like when someone is "shocked" by something they see or hear. This expression can be used to create an amusingly exaggerated reaction to a silly situation, which will get audiences laughing.

Beyond comedy, eye movements can also be used to convey subtle emotions that support a story's narrative. For example, in the movie "Gone Girl," there is a scene where Ben Affleck's character Nick Dunne conveys his guilt and sadness with only his eyes. His gaze is low and drawn inward, which mirrors his sorrow over his situation.

Wide eyes, raising eyebrows, squinting, or using other expressions in humorous ways create visuals that help sell the story to listeners, add to the humor of the story you're telling, and make your audience laugh. With practice, anyone can use eye responses effectively to create funny moments.

Facial Expression

Body language is a powerful tool for captivating audiences, especially when it comes to conveying funny moments. Facial gestures play an essential role in storytelling, helping to bring the story and characters to life. People use facial expressions to make a scene funnier, adding depth and dimension to the visuals that help sell the story to the listeners. Expressions like smirks, grins, grimaces, or frowns can convey emotion without saying a single word. This is especially true for funny people – humorous facial expressions make it easier for audiences to connect with their jokes and stories.

The psychology behind using facial gestures to add humor is quite simple; it helps build an emotional connection between the storyteller and the audience. When facial expressions are used, they draw out emotions from listeners, making them more receptive to what is being said. Using gestures lets you emphasize certain points or ideas in the story, making it more interesting. It also shows that you are passionate about what you are saying and want your audience to take notice.

Facial gestures come in many different guises, from subtle eye rolls and sly smiles to exaggerated scowls and wide-eyed shock. Consider how Jim Carrey uses his face in films like "Ace Ventura" or "Liar Liar." His physical comedy relies heavily on facial expressions ranging from dramatic to subtle and goofy to menacing.

Comedians often rely on facial gestures as well to get their jokes across. While the punchline might provide the biggest laugh, a comedian's facial expression as they deliver can also bring out a few chuckles from the audience. Similarly, while telling stories in stand-up acts or even during conversations with friends, people use facial expressions to emphasize points and draw attention to them by creating humorous visuals. Take Ellen DeGeneres, for example. Her signature wide-eyed expression often punctuates a joke with a punchline that comes out of nowhere, making it even funnier than before! Similarly, stand-up comics like Kevin Hart or Amy Schumer use exaggerated facial expressions to emphasize the humor in their routines.

Facial gestures are also useful for conveying emotions without saying anything at all. A simple wink or eyebrow raise could indicate interest or approval of something just said or done. Similarly, frowning or scowling could communicate displeasure or disappointment. This can be especially effective in comedic moments, as a well-timed facial expression can add an extra layer of hilarity to the scene. Facial gestures can also be used as part of a character's dialogue, such as when an actor adds extra emphasis on certain words or phrases by raising an eyebrow or sticking out their tongue. In TV series like "The Office" or "The Big Bang Theory," actors like Steve Carell and Jim Parsons use facial expressions to punctuate their dialogue with a comical effect.

Facial gestures play a key role in storytelling for both serious and funny people. They help add depth and dimension that help sell the story and often emphasize humorous moments by expressing emotions without having to say anything. By understanding how facial expressions work and their effect on a narrative, people can use them to create truly memorable moments that will stick with audiences for years.

Neck Responses

Neck responses are subtle movements or gestures that involve turning, jerking, or leaning one's head or neck back and forth. Storytellers can create a vivid picture for their audience by using these simple yet effective expressions and making them laugh out loud. They can be very effective in creating a comedic effect or amusing visual image for listeners of a story.

For example, you might arch your eyebrows and tilt your head slightly to express surprise in your storyline. This will let the listeners know that something unusual has happened on the scene, and they should pay attention to it. Similarly, if you want to add humor to a situation, simply tilt your chin upwards and raise your eyebrows quickly. This action will make the listeners laugh out loud.

The psychology behind using neck responses as a humorous device is that these reactions involve rapid movement, which catches people off guard and makes them laugh. By quickly turning your head away from something or someone, you create a sense of surprise for the viewer or listener, leading to an instantaneous reaction or burst of laughter.

In addition to these expressions, neck responses can be used to create different characters in a scene. A good example of this is found in the movie "The Hangover," where Zach Galifianakis uses his neck response along with the arching of one eyebrow, combined with a slight smirk, to show that he is playing a funny and mischievous character, something which adds immensely to the success of the movie. Similarly, comedians like Dave Chappelle use this technique as part of their act, jerking their heads back at certain jokes to elicit a humorous response from the audience. Often, this movement is accompanied by an eye-roll or smirk, which adds to the comedic value of the joke.

Not only are neck responses a great tool for further enhancing stories through visuals, but they are also easy to learn and perfect for a variety of situations. They are a great tool for adding visual humor to any story. They can be used to surprise, shock, and amuse listeners and viewers alike. By quickly turning one's head away from something or someone in an exaggerated manner, people can create a genuine laugh-out-loud moment that will stick with their listeners long after the story is over.

Hand Gestures

Hand and arm gestures also add a lot of visual interest to a story, making them more enjoyable for your audience and helping to sell the story. Hand and arm gestures provide visual cues that draw attention to certain aspects of the story, such as when something funny is said or done. This type of body language can help set up jokes and create an atmosphere in which laughter is more likely. In addition, these hand motions can be used to emphasize certain points or ideas during storytelling.

Hand and arm gestures can add visual interest and energy to stories involving physical activity or humorous situations. By using exaggerated hand or arm gestures for characters running, jumping, or being active, storytellers can emphasize the action taking place and create a more dynamic atmosphere. In humorous situations, hand and arm gestures can add extra emphasis to the joke by pointing out key elements of the humor to an audience. For example, if a character is telling a joke about the elephant in the room, then using exaggerated hand gestures, which could help draw attention to the size of the elephant, can make for a few laughs when done correctly.

Hand movements are especially good for making stories fun and entertaining for the listeners. Gestures like finger-pointing, waving arms around, or holding your hands together can draw people's attention to the storyteller's point. It also helps get people involved in the story by providing additional visuals for them to focus on during their listening experience.

Use appropriate hand and arm gestures to bring out the humor when telling funny stories. For example, when describing an amusing situation, you can use exaggerated hand motions to act out the scene for your audience. Comedians often use finger-pointing and raising hands in mock surprise to make their stories funnier.

In addition to helping people tell funny stories, hand and arm gestures also help convey different emotions, such as frustration or excitement. When telling a story about a character's struggles, people can use facial expressions and hand movements to express the character's feelings in a way that words cannot capture. This adds another layer of realism and helps listeners relate better to the characters in the story.

The psychology behind using body language can be quite complex. However, it is significant to remember that you should use hand and arm movements with purpose. Before using any hand and arm gestures, ask yourself why you are doing it and if it makes sense within the context of your story. That way, you can ensure your storytelling is as effective as possible.

Body language like hand and arm gestures are incredibly useful in making stories more visually appealing while conveying emotions and humor. With their help, people can get the audience involved in their stories through additional visuals for them to focus on during their listening experience. By taking some time to practice different types of hand and arm gestures, people will be able to tell better stories that look funny and entertaining!

Body Gestures

Body language can be used to create a more engaging, entertaining, and memorable story for listeners. Body gestures, when used appropriately, can add a visual element to storytelling that helps sell the story. This is especially true when it comes to comedic stories. Facial expressions, hand gestures, and other body movements create an atmosphere of humor that engages the audience and keeps them interested in the story.

Humor is largely rooted in psychology. By understanding why certain physical actions evoke laughter, we can use them to make stories funnier. One example is *exaggeration.* Stretching out one's arms or making huge eyes brings attention to a particular action or emotion and often elicits laughs from viewers. Another common technique is *facial mimicry,* such as exaggerating a character's emotions or copying the expressions of another character on stage.

Popular television shows, such as "Parks and Recreation" and "Seinfeld," use body language to bring out their funny sides. For example, in "Parks and Recreation," Leslie Knope (Amy Poehler) makes big movements with her hands while she talks, which makes everyone laugh. In Seinfeld, Jerry Seinfeld often uses facial expressions to emphasize a joke or point he is making.

We can also look to comedians for examples of how to use body language for humor. Chris Rock often works his arms wildly when telling jokes about race relations or social issues. Dave Chapelle often stands still and raises one eyebrow to punctuate his punchlines. Kevin Hart exaggerates movements to create visual representations of his jokes.

The use of body language for humor is not limited to television, movies, and stand-up comedy; it can also be used in everyday life. When telling a funny story or joke, try using big gestures to bring attention to certain aspects of the story. Use facial expressions when making points or punchlines. You can also mimic characters' physicality in your stories for added effect.

Overall, body language is essential for creating humorous stories that engage audiences. Facial expressions, hand gestures, and other body movements draw attention to critical parts of the story, making them more memorable and entertaining. By understanding the psychology behind why certain actions evoke laughter, people can use body language to make stories funnier. Examples of body language for humor can be seen in popular television shows, movies, and stand-up comedy performances. However, it can also be used in everyday life.

With a bit of practice and an understanding of why certain movements evoke laughter, anyone can use body language to add that extra comedic element to the storytelling. The results will be highly rewarding not only for you but also for your audience, who get to enjoy the compelling visuals that accompany your story.

Tips on How to Use Body Language as a Tool for Humor

1. Posture and Movement Hacks for Funny Folks

Using body language such as posture and movement is a great way to add humor to any conversation. Posture can drastically change the tone of interaction and even make others laugh when executed correctly. For instance, leaning in closely and dramatically when revealing a secret or joke shows that what you are saying is very important, which increases suspense and often elicits laughter. Purposefully awkward movements can also prove comical. Actors and comedians know that exaggerated gestures like abrupt twitches contribute to much of the humor in their performances. Even seemingly mundane tasks like standing up, walking across a room, or going through daily routines can become comedic when done with enthusiasm, whether serious or not. With just a few quick hacks, funny folks can easily use body language to increase the laugh factor of their interactions!

2. Shifting Your Weight and Pacing

Body language plays an integral part in many people's sense of humor. Have you ever noticed that a performer on a stage might shift their weight from one foot to the other or even pace back and forth? It's no coincidence. They're making use of their physicality as a form of comedic expression. This type of body language has been shown to effectively communicate humor in ways that conversation alone is sometimes unable to accomplish; it's all about control. As funny folks can attest, controlling your body movements, like shifting your weight or pacing, can be invaluable when it comes to cracking up a crowd or hitting just the right comedic timing. So why not practice such skills? You may find that they help you become more confident and effective when telling jokes, creating sketches, or improvising with others. It's time to break out those funny bones, activate those locomotive muscles, and explore these techniques for yourself!

3. Facial Expressions

A great way to add humor to any situation is through *facial expressions*. Raising your eyebrows, making a silly face, or even widening your eyes can all make for an effective joke delivery system!

4. Gestures

Body language is an invaluable asset for people who strive to be funny and to bring humor into conversations. Whether you're trying to induce laughter or add a comedic element to your words, body language is the vital missing piece of the puzzle. Hand gestures, facial expressions, and stances can all be used in conjunction with speech to further emphasize jokes, stories, and exaggerations. The use of body language to establish humor also encourages people in conversation to become comfortable with one another and engage in more lively banter. From leaning in towards a person and widening their eyes for humorous results to using relaxed arm movements for added comical effect, there are many tips that funny folks can employ when using body language hacks as a tool.

5. Pacing

Pacing is another very effective tool for funny folks to keep their audience entertained. By varying their delivery from slowing down during punchlines to speeding up when introducing topics, funny folks can keep the conversation interesting and engage with the audience more effectively. This practice will capture attention better and add inflection and emotion, which are hard to convey with facial expressions and hand gestures alone. By controlling the speed at which they speak, funny people are able to engineer laughter in their listeners through an intentional method of speaking. When all other elements of humor fall short or don't quite hit home with the listener, the pacing is often what turns good jokes into great ones. Whether someone is a beginner storyteller looking to find their funny groove or an experienced comedian on stage honing their comedic skills, mastering the art of pacing can have huge benefits for a comic's repertoire.

By using these tips on how to use body language as a tool for humor, you'll be sure to get those good laughs you've been looking for! With some practice, timing, and confidence, it won't be long before you're making people chuckle with every move you make!

Chapter 7: The Golden Key to an Unforgettable Joke

Making a good first impression, captivating an audience, or selling an idea or story to a specific group of people does not always have to involve your outfit, social status, or the event's convener. It could be as simple as a great joke or a clear storyline. One punchline, a great story, or an epiphany could make the audience laugh, pay attention to you, and fixate on the message you're trying to convey.

Some people may not be naturally inclined to tell stories or make jokes, making it difficult for them to capture an audience or maintain conversations. One of the simplest ways to break the ice or draw your audience's attention is humor. While it may not be easy, there are ways to inject some fun into your story or speech.

Mastering the art of storytelling is integral to captivating an audience.
https://www.pexels.com/photo/laughing-asian-male-skaters-resting-on-street-staircase-5368963/

Vivid imagery effectively appeals to a crowd and keeps your message or joke in their memory. Over the years, it has been used by both comedians and the best storytellers. Attaching an image to a story or joke helps the listener remember the joke for years to come thus, vivid imagery is "the golden key" to an unforgettable joke.

Vivid imagery involves language that appeals to our senses to help a listener or reader visualize and comprehend the author's message. It entails employing descriptive words, images, or scenarios, so the listener or reader understands what you're saying. It means capturing the listener's attention and imagination with descriptive, detailed, and powerful words or images to make the sentence more vivid.

Creating intense images to match and describe the characters and setting of your story is part of telling a joke or telling a story using vivid imagery. You're providing context for the listeners and making sure your characters sound alive and believable. Every word counts because it links to stimulating your listeners' mental imaging.

Storytelling has deep roots in our society and has played a crucial role in transmitting morals, skills, and behaviors through the ages. The listener can paint a picture of the story using imagery, making it impossible to forget. People can recall a joke for years to come when words have been drawn into an image and have stuck in their memory.

Seven Ways of Using Vivid Imagery in Storytelling or Joke Making

The key to an unforgettable joke or story is in the details and how vivid they are for listeners to remember. Creating an image or setting for a story can be challenging, but here are a few tips to help you achieve this:

1. Ensure Clarity

Think about clarity before sharing your story or attempting to impress the audience. The importance of clarity in storytelling helps the audience understand your story. Use simple language to lead your readers through the story rather than confusing components, which will distort their perception of the story.

Clarity enables you to pay attention to the feelings and emotions of your audience. It would be simpler for your audience to comprehend your story if you used straightforward language rather than ambiguous terminology or buzzwords. When you use several terms, you risk confusing your audience and obfuscating their understanding of your words.

Use terms they are accustomed to hearing - words that are important to their culture or that their age groups use frequently. Some idioms could be vulgar, insulting, or out of date. Consider your audience's reaction to your words, then exploit it to draw them in.

2. Use Figurative Language

A great technique for storytellers who wish to keep their audience interested is figurative language. Vivid imagery is all about using figures of speech that appeal to our five senses to explain every element of your scene, characters, and activities in the story.

There isn't much room to give the listener an image, but figurative language enables powerful images in a limited space. Similes, metaphors, analogies, and rhetorical questions are examples of figurative language that enhance the meaning of words. Your audience will be better able to see what is being described and absorb it deeper.

The linking and comparing items using "as" and "like." For instance, "the moment I saw my family, I felt peace like a still flowing river" implies that the character was at peace with himself when they mentioned their family, but comparing it to a "still flowing river" sheds more light on the character's feeling of peace and provides the reader with more insight into the character's actions.

While metaphoric words combine two things and discover a link, a rhetorical question requires the audience to think rather than respond. Analogies and sarcastic remarks are also amusing ways to put your audience's mental imaging to the test.

The objective is to establish a strong impression for the audience by connecting two facts or ideas. Using figurative language in your storytelling gives your audience a more thorough understanding of your tale. Linking the words to relatable or cultural expressions in your audience's horizon helps them grasp the full context of your story, leaving it in their memory forever.

3. Use Concrete Descriptions

Clarity and concrete language will help the reader understand your story better. Eliminate words from your story that are not necessary and weaken its impact. Vivid imagery means drawing more attention to your setting and character, so don't be afraid to use strong language in your description.

When describing something, you should use one strong phrase rather than several and be specific in your word choice to avoid ambiguity. Avoid using words like "extremely" and "very" wherever possible. You will also find using action verbs whenever possible and excluding superfluous filler useful.

Don't be scared to describe something in more depth. Instead of just calling a woman beautiful, describing her as having a porcelain complexion, woolly hair, and crystal blue eyes are more descriptive and visual. Don't be afraid to be specific, but know when it's too much.

4. Create Surprising Contrasts

Surprise elements in storytelling are a good way to keep your listeners on the edge of their seats and interested in the story. If they know what to expect, the story becomes boring, and your joke loses its humor. However, introducing contrasts and unexpected twists allows for vivid imagery.

One example is to describe things in unexpected ways. If you've heard two people tell the same story and it sounds completely different, you've experienced the power of vivid imagery. They understand the standard description, but what if they saw it in a different light? Be original, one-of-a-kind, and deliberate in your description to give listeners and readers a new and refined perspective on your characters.

5. The Active Voice

Wooing an audience will be difficult if the storyteller is not intentionally describing the elements in their story or making the story come alive. This means telling a story using the active forms of a verb. In your story, the voice describes who is the doer or receiver of an action, and using the active voice means emphasizing the subject or doer of the activity. Rather than saying, "The ball was passed from the striker to the midfielder, and it was struck in the net," an active form would sound like this, "The striker passed the ball to the midfielder who struck the ball past the keeper into the back of the net." When telling a story or joke, you want to sound unique and as interested in it as your listener.

Starting sentences with a subjective verb adds action, activity, and interest. Using the active voice is a good place to start if you want to keep your audience engaged and focused on your message.

6. Use Appropriate Emotions

Nothing influences a character's mood or actions more than emotions. Emotions affect the setting and perceptions of characters, and the listeners feel it. Emotions enable them to perceive a character, draw conclusions, and eventually follow the story.

As a storyteller, you must be aware of your emotions and their impact on your story. Your real-world audience will see your characters as static images if they lack emotions or feelings, and you will fail to capture their attention. Once you understand your characters' emotions, you can use them to entertain your audience.

7. Character Revelation

Character revelation is one of the most important aspects of vivid imagery that keeps your listeners focused. The way you reveal your characters influences how they perceive it. Instead of telling your characters, show them.

Don't just tell what's going on; use words and actions to reveal the character. An actor's body language, muscular and facial compression, and short blunt answers reveal and show the person's anger. It is critical to be accurate while also bringing balance to the character by not using too much detail. Recognize when it is enough to avoid overwhelming the listener.

Vivid imagery is a difficult but necessary tool for telling an unforgettable story or joke. It may be the golden key you seek, but using it requires attention to detail, accuracy, and versatility.

Make your storyline clear. Keep it simple, carefully detailed, and concise to avoid ambiguity. You don't want to bore the listeners with too much detail. Utilize your surroundings to make the most of your limited space.

Be deliberate in your storytelling. Tell it in a way that the listeners haven't heard before. Allow them to experience the world through the eyes of your characters. Take advantage of their sensitivity and perception by using a sensitive description. Don't use offensive, archaic, or colloquial expressions. Examine them and take note of any feedback.

Keep the element of surprise in mind. Listeners may find your story boring or flat if it follows the expected path or contains a lot of clichés. Use an active voice and strong words to keep them on edge. Don't be afraid to remove any unnecessary words that reduce your description's power. Avoid redundancy and capitalize on the power of emotions and time. Use figurative language and combine elements wisely to create a vivid image for your audience.

Nine Tips to Improve Your Storytelling Skills

Storytelling is deeply ingrained in our culture. It has been used to teach and pass skills to younger generations and sell a thought or idea to a group of people.

Storytelling has helped to engage people, explain various concepts and perspectives, and give readers or listeners a glimpse into new worlds. Stories have broadened people's minds and helped them gain deeper and more meaningful insights into themselves and the world.

Storytelling is a dynamic tool that can inspire and educate millions of people. Some people can fully use storytelling, while others cannot. It can be challenging to engage an audience with a good narrative, so here are nine tips to help you improve:

1. A Clear Message

The story's core is your message, that is, the point you're trying to make and convey to the listeners. Your audience will remember the message because that is what the story is about. Knowing what message you're trying to convey gives you direction as you write or speak.

Have a clear understanding of the story's message or focal point, regardless of the genre. The story will progress with such a message if it is morally based. In the case of a joke, twists and puns are added to keep the audience entertained. If the story is compelling, the appropriate amount of drama and suspense is developed from the beginning to the climax.

2. Have a Structure

Aside from the story's direction or main point, it requires a proper structure. There are numerous ways to structure your story, but it must have a beginning, a middle (or body), and an ending. This gives you the framework on which to build the suspense or energy of the previous sections of the story and end on a strong note. You'll be able to keep your audience interested from beginning to end.

Your structure could serve as a guide for your story. It provides a proper sequence for the audience to follow, bringing the curtain down with a satisfying resolution. Your structure will assist in guiding your audience and preparing the format in which you intend to tell the story.

3. Engage the Audience

A great storyteller captivates their audience. Being a good storyteller is telling a good story – *and telling it in a good way.* You must first understand your audience and devise a compelling way to tell the story to them. The style of storytelling you use influences how attentive your audience will be.

Make eye contact and use body language when talking to a group of people. You will feel liberated and less nervous and engage your listeners, who will keep their gaze fixed on you, the storyteller.

You should also express your emotions through your voice and allow your expressiveness to flow through it. Make gestures and express yourself to keep your audience entertained.

4. Embrace Conflict

Higher intelligence is a distinguishing feature of humans. Our ability to brainstorm, adapt to challenges, solve problems, and find solutions is extremely impressive. You can use this narrative as a storyteller. Test your audience's mental fortitude and watch them respond with delight.

Great storytellers embrace conflict and use it to pique their audience's or reader's interest. Keeping it too simple or direct can be boring, so embrace conflict. Start your first paragraph with a perplexing situation or question. It will make listeners think and be interested in the story's remaining parts/outcome.

5. Using Vivid Details

Using vivid details is a characteristic shared by many great storytellers. Highly descriptive words and details are used to pique the readers' interest. Details add imagery to your story and make a significant difference.

Storytelling is a great way to take your audience from the known to the unknown. You can help them understand difficult subjects by explaining unfamiliar concepts. To help your listeners connect with the characters and immerse themselves in the story, use tiny details to describe them.

Color, taste, smell, or touch details will have them hooked. Make sure to use these details to keep them interested in your story.

6. Use Personal Experiences

Personalizing your story increases its uniqueness and originality. Telling your listeners about personal experiences that you have had and turning them into a story will pique their interest. They'll feel more connected, listen with greater enthusiasm and intent, and have a greater impact. You can always turn personal experiences into stories, whether it's your story or not.

7. Make It Relatable

Humans are receptive beings who prefer ideas they already have an interest in. People are drawn to ideas they find relatable, and there is no better feeling than knowing your audience understands your story or area of interest.

Many books become best-sellers due to the relativity factor. They are focused on relatable topics that pique the audience's interest. If you're selling your or someone else's story, make it relatable and general to the audience.

Through your story or character, you can present the world or yourself. When your audience can relate to the topic, you'll get a lot of positive feedback and interest. Allow the story to feel like theirs.

8. Ensure Brevity

Could you keep it simple, short, and to the point? People in today's fast-paced world want key details. To keep your audience engaged, avoid overloading them with unnecessary information. Keep the important and entertaining information at the heart of the story. Please don't waste your words. Instead, include details where they are relevant. Details bring the story to life, but too many details bore the listener. Keep it short.

9. Observe Other Storytellers

Observation is a great way to learn. You have a unique story, but you can improve your storytelling skills by watching how others do it. Observing people whom we regard as eloquent and masterful storytellers can help us learn to be better storytellers.

Watching other storytellers can teach you techniques, communication styles, and how to craft a story. You could learn how to use a technique to its full potential and easily reach your target audience by paying close attention to another storyteller.

Storytelling is a wonderful art. It can simplify the most complex topics and tell people a captivating story. It takes practice to convey a message to listeners through a story, but with the right tips and information, you'll be a better storyteller in no time.

Five Ways to Improve Your Sense of Humor

Storytelling and good humor are great ways to keep your audience's attention. You'll captivate them and fill your story with energy to keep them interested from beginning to end.

In our everyday lives, humor is highly valued. Life can be amusing, and a good sense of humor can make it even more so. Being funny can help with social interactions and turn a gloomy situation into a fun one, but not everyone knows how to tell a good joke or has a good sense of humor.

Being amusing is a valuable skill that can be applied in various situations. If you don't have a great sense of humor, don't worry; a few simple tips will help you improve.

1. See the Funny Side

If you're trying to become more humorous, try to see the lighter side of things. Consider things from a different angle. It's a useful skill to have when trying to be a jokester. Look for the amusing or hidden joke in things. Just try it - if you're stressed, include some levity.

2. Learn Simple Jokes

You don't have to be particularly creative to improve your sense of humor. Learn a few jokes, search the internet, watch comedic shows or clips, and put a few jokes you've learned into practice. Try it in front of a small group or during a conversation. If it doesn't work immediately, keep trying and switch up your jokes.

3. Be Positive and Laugh More

What you don't have, you can't give. You can't make others happy if you're unhappy. See the lighter side of things, express some joy, and making others happy won't be difficult. When you're in a good mood, a couple of jokes will rumble in you, and if you let them out, everyone will laugh. People will laugh at your jokes if you exude positive energy.

4. Be Witty, Not Giddy

It's okay to start with silly humor for some audiences, but it quickly turns sour. Silly jokes may make you appear immature, but it never goes out of style. Wit extends beyond stale jokes and sarcasm.

To become wittier, one must combine delightful ideas with creative spontaneity. Once you are comfortable making witty remarks, you can try it in the real world to boost your sense of humor by jesting with a more humorous person and overcoming nervousness.

5. Don't Overdo It

There is a fine line between being amusing and offensive. Making humorous remarks could be entertaining to one audience but offensive to another. Understand your target audience's mood or disposition. To avoid conflicts, make jokes about yourself whenever possible or about things that people can change. Making witty remarks and employing sarcasm is valuable, but know when to stop.

Captivating an audience is essential for communicating and spreading ideas. It's a quality that good storytellers have mastered over the years. It takes great skill to break down complex issues and speak to an audience while keeping them enthralled by the story.

Many comedians and storytellers use vivid imagery to capture the attention of their audiences. It could be the key to an unforgettable joke or story. It entails using concrete descriptors, figurative language, active voicing, and surprise to keep the audience engaged in the story and paint a lasting image.

The story must be clear, free of ambiguity, and suspenseful to keep listeners entertained. The listener must understand the underlying message to create a lasting image. A good joke or story would benefit from adding good humor and human mental capacity.

The importance of conciseness and clarity cannot be overstated. A joke or story is more interesting to its audience when it is accurate and balanced. A good combination of excellent storytelling and a sense of humor will provide the listener with an unforgettable experience.

Chapter 8: Proven Jokes That Will Make Anyone Laugh

When you hear a short, hilarious joke, you can't help but laugh out loud. Although some may seem silly, you can always find humor. Even the most hilarious jokes are subjective and do not appeal to everyone. Both the delivery and reception of a joke will influence its viability.

Having a good time with other people is always more fun. Did you know, however, that it can also benefit your health? Laughter triggers the body's natural relaxation response.

Laughter boosts your immune system, improves your mood, alleviates your pain, and protects you from the damaging effects of stress. It is a potent medicine. It connects individuals in a way that induces positive physical and emotional changes in the body.

When we were younger, we frequently laughed. Now that we're adults, we take life more seriously and laugh less. Looking for more comedy and laughter opportunities helps strengthen relationships, be happier, and even live longer.

These amusing short jokes are certain to make you laugh! Since laughter is the best medicine, share it with others to make their days a little brighter.

Here are the best-categorized jokes to make people laugh:

Geography Jokes

- Why does Yeti recognize all of the map signs?
  Because it is a legend!

- Student: I'll never be an expert in geography.
  Geographer: Not with that latitude.

- What did the rock say to the photographer?
  Don't take me for Granite!

- Mountains aren't just funny...
  They are hill-areas!

- What do mountains see
  They peak!

- Geology is important, but geography is the real deal.
  What did the tectonic plates say when they collided?
  My apologies!

- What rock band has four people that don't even sing?
  Mount Rushmore

- Johnny is seated in geography.
  He suddenly extends his hand.
  "Yes," the teacher says. "Excuse me, teacher, but I was wondering if the Earth is flat."
  The instructor turns to face him and responds, visibly annoyed, "No, not at all. Any other silly questions?"
  "Yes," Johnny responds. How could The Dead Sea pass away?

- Would you like to hear a geography joke?
  Hey, Tom, if you're in Hungary, let me bring you a turkey sandwich, Bob said.
  "That was a terrible joke, Oman." - Tom.
  "I know Yemen," - Bob.
  Syriasly, you should stop making these jokes - Tom.
  But Iraq is good at making jokes - Bob.

- I'm not very good at geography.

  But I know the name of one city in France, which is Nice.
- I once dated a teacher.

  Initially, there was *chemistry* between us.

  It was *history* for both of us at the time of our breakup.

  We now have *geographic* distance because she moved away.
- My son got an F on his geography exam today.

  When I told him to go to his room, he went to the kitchen instead.
- Guess what the beach said to the tide?

  Long time no sea!
- I have a Geography joke but I don't know where it is
- Which country do you think is the coldest?

  Chile
- How does the Ocean greets?

  It waves.
- What is the name given to a colorful atmospheric anomaly that arises above Barcelona?

  A Spainbow!
- A student threatens his English teacher with a gun. "Give me all of your cash, or you are geography!"

  You mean history, right?

  "Do not change the subject!"
- I should review my knowledge of geography.

  My new television came with the words "Built-In Antenna" written on it. I'm not sure where *Antenna* is.
- My wife only has one problem. She doesn't know the difference between geography and geology.

  Regardless, she still rocks my world.
- I overheard my son praying, "God bless Mommy and Daddy, and please make Hamburg the capital of Germany," as I passed by his bedroom.

Why do you want Hamburg to become Germany's capital, son?" I inquired.

"Because that's the answer I decided to write in my geography test," he replied as he turned to face me.

Pun Jokes

- I tried to make a carpentry pun with that woodwork.

  I think I nailed it!

- Puns come in two varieties.

  There are puns that are amusing to hear and puns that are irritating.

- Why did this penguin use a fish pun?

  Only to get the halibut.

- A horrible pun

  What is the favorite dish of a mathematician?

  Pie

- A man chose to enter his neighborhood newspaper's pun competition. He submitted ten puns in the hopes that one would be chosen.

  Unfortunately, not one of the ten puns worked.

Several hilarious puns:

- What is the name of a cow without legs?

  Minced beef.

- What is the name of a cow that only has one leg?

  Steak!

- What is the name of a cow with two legs?

  Lean meat!

- What is the name of a three-legged cow?

  The tri-tip.

- What's the name of a four-legged cow?

  Of course, a cow!

- Hey, you've been a little dark lately, says the moon. That seems to contradict your entire soul's goal. When are you going to stop telling me these lune-atic puns? asks the sun in response.

- Where have all the clever chemistry puns gone?

  Argon has the most inventive chemistry.

- I once competed in a weather pun contest and defeated the winning raining champion.

- I'm going to write 10000000 binary puns to follow the pattern of binary puns.

  Update: On occasion, I bite far more than I can chew.

- Why can't you coexist with trees?

  Because they will leaf

- I'm attempting to make a yoga-related pun, but it's not working.

  Of course, it's a stretch.

- I've got a space pun.

  However, I require a little more time to planet.

Literature Jokes

- What would be Socrates favorite item to mold?

  A play dough (Plato)!

- What would we find in the pantry of Charles Dickens?

  The best of thyme and the worst of thyme.

- Choosing which pencil to use for the English literature test is proving difficult.

  This is the dilemma: 2B or not 2B?

- I used to work as a translator of ancient Greek literature into Braille.

  It appears to be ancient history.

- Penguin Books appears to only publish esoteric literature...

  They only see things in black and white.

- Literature for escalators.

  A guide to advancing to new levels.

- Obesity poses a serious threat to public health.

  There is a growing body of literature on this topic.

- What did Arithmetic textbook say to the literature text?
  You are full of amazing stories and I'm full of problems.

Language Jokes

- I don't mean to brag, but I speak ten languages fluently.
  Binary and English.
- What is the least spoken language in the world?
  Sign language.
- What is the term for someone who is trilingual or more?
  Multilingual.
- Some people believe that learning English is difficult.
  You can handle it through thorough thought, though.
- Are there any words that has all five vowels and a Y?
  Unquestionably!
- I've decided to learn sign language so that I can learn jokes that have never been told before.
- Why are pirates unable to use sign language?
  Because the hook presents everything as a query.
- What would you call an antelope without eyes in sign language?
  Whatever you desire. You can't see it.
- What did Oedipus' father say when he heard him use profanity?
  I'm hoping you won't kiss your mother with that mouth of yours.
- Two polyglots and language nerds meet in a bar:
  Hey, how are things going?
  - Nothing new here, just polishing my Finnish... how about you?
  - As you are aware, I am nearly finished with my Polish.
- She is reading a book on antigravity.
  She can't put it down.

- After showing me around her apartment, my date said, "Make yourself at home."

  She requested that I leave because English was not her first language.

- What is the longest word in English?

  Smiles. Each S is separated by one mile.

- What happened to the room when the present, past, and future walked in?

  It was tense.

- Wife: What is your least favorite aspect of the English language?

  Husband: Personal pronoun in the second person singular

  Wife: What?

  Husband: YOU.

- I kissed her after she continued to fix her gaze on my lips.

  To cut a long story short, I'm currently learning sign language.

- The word frequently is one of my favorites in the English language.

  I try to use it as much as possible.

- My son is yelling, "Duck! Duck! Duck!" as he walks through the house.

  I warned him to stop using such fowl language.

- According to an English professor, there are no positive words in the English language that denote a negative. However, two negatives can also mean a positive.

  The back row of the class: "Yea. Right!"

- I went on a date with someone who could also speak Zulu, and we hit it off right away.

- An amusing joke I translated from the original language:

  A man is walking through a cemetery at night when he notices a woman sitting near a grave.

  He approaches her out of concern and inquires as to why she is seated so close to a grave.

"I came out because I was hot inside," the woman responds.

- The teacher asked Nora to mention two pronouns.
  She said, "Who, me?"

- A-Cyrillic is the language of Slavic painters.

Nature Jokes

- Happy belated Mother's Day, Mother Nature!
  I would have said it out loud yesterday, but she grounded me.

- I believe Nature enjoys humiliation.
  The worse we handle it, the hotter it gets.

- I had to take an important call, so I was late for a family dinner.

- Gravity is very important as the first and most powerful natural force.
  If you throw it out, you get gravy.

- Why do geckos naturally tell stories?
  Their nature is to drop a tail.

- What did one leaf say to the other leaf?
  I'm falling for you.

- Why was the scarecrow awarded?
  Because he was exceptional in his field.

- What do you call someone who is so terrified of nature that they will go to any length to try to control it?
  An organic chicken.

- Why they bother teaching science history concepts in a lesson like "Nature abhors a void" is beyond me.
  Everyone who has ever had a pet understands this.

- When possible, hike through nature with an experienced hiker.
  Bears find new hikers bland and tasteless.

- Did you know that the color blue does not exist in nature?
  It's all a figment of your imagination

- What did the spider check on the internet?
  He checked his website.

- What did the big flower say to the small flower?

  Hey, bud!

Sports Jokes

- What do you call a boat full of well-mannered football players?

  Excellent Sportsmanship

- Why does Cinderella struggle with sports?

  She takes off after the ball. Her coach is also a vegetable.

- A sports store is holding a competition to see who can hit punching bags the hardest to promote its new punching bags.

  As everyone waits for their turn, St. Peter turns to one of the drunks and says, "I believe I'm in the false joke."

  The response was, "Nope. Simply put, the punch line was incorrect."

- Which sports do waiters excel at?

  Tennis. They have received excellent service training.

- I am frequently asked to pose for photographs for sports magazines, articles on diet-related topics, men's health, etc.

  The person in the "before" photos is me.

- Why was the golfer dressed in two pants?

  Just in case he gets a hole in one.

- Where is New York City's largest diamond kept?

  Yankee Stadium.

- What would you call a French sports car?

  A Baguetti

- An arsonist should not participate in sports.

  They throw matches all the time.

- How is a pickpocket different from an umpire?

  One steals watches and one watches steals.

- Why are baseball matches always played in the nighttime?

  Because the bat was sleeping during the day.

Car Jokes

- Someone is wanted for stealing the police car's wheels.

  The police are searching for the suspect nonstop.

- A police vehicle stops a man after nearly colliding with two cars.

  "Can I please see your license?" the officer inquired. After searching his belongings, he hands over his license to the officer. "Sir, according to your license, you must wear glasses while driving."

  "Oh, I didn't see that," the man said.

- It's odd that the town in the Cars movie is called "Radiator Springs," considering that a radiator is primarily a vital organ for a car.

  That's like having a city called "Liver Pool" for humans.

- A century ago, only the wealthy had access to automobiles, and everyone rode horses to work.

  Today, only the wealthy can afford horses, and everyone drives a car.

  Oh, how the stables have changed.

- Why did Volkswagen wait until last year to begin producing electric vehicles in the United States?

  Because it took them some time to iron out the bugs.

- Why can't computers drive cars?

  As a result of frequent crashes

Food Jokes

- Let's face it, if I were hungry, I'd talk about food, so I make a lot of jokes about women.

- I'm tired of hearing how bad British food is. Any other country's cuisine is the world's second most delectable, with French cuisine coming in first.

- What happens when you cross a turbocharger and a chicken?
  Fast food

- A food critic attempted to steal pie-making recipes while rating and assessing pies from various bakeries.

  Pie-rating was what she did.

- Aldi's low prices don't just apply to food.

  They only cost quarters and have shopping carts!

- My grandmother enjoys making us laugh by pretending to choke on food.

  It was an old joke.

- Have you heard the sad story about the guy who sat in food dye?

  He eventually dyed.

- My friend claims that onions are the only food that can make him cry.

  Then, I smashed him in the face with a watermelon.

- What piques the interest of the British sea creature?

  Ships and fish

- Where can spirits get food?

  The ghostery store

- Why don't eggs tell jokes?

  Because they're afraid they'd crack each other up.

- What did the bacon say to the tomato?

  Lettuce get-together!

- How should I eat when I have a cold?

  I, I, I, CHHHHHEEEWWWWWWW

- Why did the cookie go to the doctor?

  Because it was feeling crumbly.

- My wife allegedly dumped me because of my food addiction.

  While I was distracted, she made a remark about not having enough thyme for herself.

- I made a joke about how much pilots enjoy their food: "They like it, plane."

- I ordered some German food online.

  The wurst is still on its way, but the sauerkraut is here!

- People who eat snails should not eat fast food.

- A man enters a restaurant.

  The waitress inquires about the man's lunch preferences, and he orders the

  rabbit stew.

  The waitress returns with his food, and he replies: "Sorry, but I believe there's a hare in the soup!"

Chapter 9: Wondrous Ways to Enhance Your Wit... Jokes Aside

As someone who loves to laugh and crack a joke, you're already familiar with the various techniques and tricks to tell a funny joke on the spot. But what about when it comes to enhancing your wit and charisma in everyday conversations? Learning to be funny isn't just about telling jokes; it's about developing a wonderful sense of humor that can help you in every aspect of life.

This chapter will look at some great tips you can apply daily to ensure that your wit and charisma are always on point! From refining your comedic skills to honing your timing and delivery, there's plenty here to help you become the wittiest and most charming person in any conversation.

Focus on your charm to be witty and to be a hit when you tell jokes.
https://www.pexels.com/photo/happy-diverse-couples-laughing-in-park-3777727/

Being Witty Isn't Just about Telling Jokes

Firstly, it's important to realize that being funny isn't all about telling jokes. Developing a witty side to your conversations means being quick-thinking and having a sharp tongue. It's about finding ways to make subtle jokes amid more serious discussions and using wordplay to your advantage. It's about being able to think of the perfect thing to say at just the right moment and knowing that it will bring a smile to everyone's face.

If you want to become the funniest and most charming person in any room, you must refine your comedy skills. It's not always natural to be witty and charismatic, but it's a skill that can be developed with practice. Here are some tips for honing your wit.

Become a Master of Quick Thinking

The first step to developing and honing your wit is to become a quick thinker. It's not just about learning how to think on the spot and come up with clever puns or witty remarks but being able to process information quickly.

Utilize Brainstorming Techniques

Brainstorming is a great way to come up with ideas on the spot. It can help you generate new and exciting concepts that you haven't thought of before. To practice brainstorming, start by thinking of a situation or topic and then quickly jot down as many ideas and thoughts as possible. This will help you become a quicker thinker, which is essential if you want to develop your wit. You can brainstorm by yourself or in a group, depending on what kind of situation you're in.

Name Objects Around You

Start by naming objects around you as quickly as possible. Don't worry about being correct or making witty comments; just quickly name whatever comes to mind first! You can make the game more interesting by challenging yourself to make unexpected associations between the things you name. This can be done by adding a mundane topic and an unexpected twist. Here are a few tips to help you make unexpected associations.

Look at things from a different perspective. Instead of looking at the world through the same lens, try to look at it from a different perspective. This can help you make unexpected connections and create new jokes.

Take a step back. By taking a step back and looking at the big picture, you can understand how different topics are related and form new perspectives. You'll see connections that you have missed by looking at them too closely – and will have fun with mundane tasks.

Think outside the box. Be bold and think outside the box. Don't be afraid to come up with comments that might seem crazy or far-fetched. They may end up being the funniest ones!

Take a break. Take a break if you're stuck and need help to come up with new jokes. Walk away from the problem for a while and return to it with a fresh perspective.

Once you get comfortable with this exercise, start making word associations, this is essential in developing your quick-thinking skills. Try coming up with words related to the objects or people around you, as this will help you develop creative observations and witty remarks faster.

Practice Regularly

To hone your wit, practice regularly. Try to find a few minutes every day to work on your ability to think quickly. By naming objects around you or coming up with word associations, you will gradually become more comfortable and confident in coming up with humorous remarks at the drop of a hat.

Playing word games like Scrabble or Boggle is also a great way to get your brain into gear and become a faster thinker. These games are fun and can help you develop interesting word combinations and new ideas.

Refining Your Comedy Skills

While it seems clichéd, practice and repetition are key to developing a sense of humor. Whether through stand-up comedy or having conversations with friends, the more you invest in honing your comedic skills, the more you refine your wit and be better equipped to respond cleverly. Improvising is extremely helpful. Not only will it help you think quickly and come up with sharp responses, but it can add a certain flair of unpredictability.

Unlock Your Inner Comedian: Take Improv Classes!

To take your joke-telling to the next level, consider taking improv (improvisation) theatre classes. Improv theatre teaches you how to think on your feet and come up with quick, witty responses. It can help you become more confident in front of an audience and better understand their reactions.

In improv classes, you'll work in groups to create scenes and characters on the spot. This exercise builds trust between group members and encourages everyone to think quickly and creatively. You'll learn how to use your body language and facial expressions to convey meaning and create humorous situations.

Listen to Your Instructor

It's essential to listen to your instructor and take their advice seriously. Improv theatre is a skill that needs to be learned, so you must understand the basics before trying to be funny. Listening carefully and paying attention in class will help you develop your quick wit and become more successful at improv comedy.

Take Risks

Improv theatre is about pushing yourself out of your comfort zone and testing the boundaries of your creativity. Don't be afraid to make mistakes, as this will help you become more experienced with improvisation, and you'll improve over time.

Have Fun

Above all else, improv theatre classes should be enjoyable. Don't take yourself too seriously, but try to relax and have fun! Ensure you are comfortable with the material, and don't hesitate to ask questions if you need help. This will help you become more confident in your ability and make the whole experience more enjoyable.

Practicing Comedy in the Mirror

Practicing comedy in the mirror is a great way to test your comedic timing and build confidence. To do this, simply stand in front of a full-length mirror and start talking as if you were on stage. This will help you become more comfortable with your material and get used to delivering it with humor and style.

Start by reciting a few jokes or funny stories that you've written. Pay attention to your facial expressions and body language as you do so. Are you conveying the emotion of the joke correctly? Are you laughing along with the audience in your head? These are all crucial elements of comedic timing that can be improved by practicing in front of the mirror. Ensure you're speaking slowly and clearly, which will help you better communicate your jokes.

Once you've practiced telling a few jokes, try improvising some scenarios in the mirror. This builds your confidence and makes it easier for you to think on your feet. It also lets you experiment with different styles and humor types without an audience.

Spend some time analyzing your performance in the mirror. Did you feel confident? Did your timing feel natural and smooth? Did you make any mistakes or need to remember what to say? This is a great way to identify areas for improvement and become more comfortable with improv comedy.

Laughing with Strangers

Remember that charisma and wit don't just come from inside the four walls of your house. They can be found in everyday encounters with strangers. Whether on the bus, in a cafe, or at the office, you never know when you might bump into someone with a great sense of humor. Try to be open and friendly. You never know what interesting conversations might arise. This can be intimidating, but it's a great way to learn how to read an audience and figure out what kind of jokes work best with different people.

When talking to someone new, ask questions that draw them out and make them laugh. Start with light, funny topics. Don't dive straight into the deep end and start telling jokes. Instead, start with light, funny topics and banter to break the ice.

The trick is having an easygoing attitude and being willing to engage in lighthearted, humorous conversation. Surround yourself with people who want to laugh, and make sure that you always have a joke or two up your sleeve. A good humorous attitude can break down barriers, open minds, and help people connect meaningfully.

Listen carefully and watch their body language so you can pick up on any quirks or interests they have. Make sure you're in a place where people are likely to be in the mood for laughing. The atmosphere is vital. It can be difficult to get the conversation going if it's too loud or too quiet.

Forget the age-old advice of "always be yourself" – it's actually much more efficient to tailor your humor to different situations and people. Be aware of other cultures and styles of humor, so you don't offend anyone or come across as insensitive. Letting your charisma and wit shine in the conversation is a great way to make a lasting impression.

Laughing with strangers is an art form; it takes practice, patience, and willingness to learn. But it can be incredibly rewarding, and you'll make new friends along the way, practice your wit, and may even learn something.

Watching Sitcoms and Comedies to Improve Wit

TV shows, films, and stand-up comedy specials are wonderful sources of entertainment. They can be great learning opportunities for budding comedians! Watching sitcoms and comedies can help you develop your wit and become a better joke-teller.

Timing is everything. Pay attention to the timing of jokes when watching sitcoms and comedies – it is essential for successfully telling a joke. Look at the way comedians deliver their punchlines, as well as how audiences react. Understanding the timing of jokes can help you deliver them perfectly when telling your own.

As you watch, note how comedians structure and deliver their jokes. Look for patterns in how they interact with one another and subtle little nuances that will help you hone your joke-telling skills. This will help you to better understand the dynamics of joke-telling and how to get a laugh.

Don't be afraid to imitate how comedians deliver their jokes – this can be a great way to practice your delivery. Studying successful comedians will give you a deeper insight into how jokes are crafted and delivered. Take note of the tone, word choice, and timing, as all of these factors contribute to making a joke funny. This will help you create better jokes and become more successful at improvisation.

An Obvious Remark

Seeing humor in everyday situations is one of the best ways to sharpen your wit. Pay attention to the little things around you and remark on them when appropriate. For example, if someone is wearing an interesting outfit, comment on it! This will demonstrate your wit and elicit a funny response.

Try to be observant and pay attention to your environment. This will help you become more adept at improvisation and make it easier to come up with witty remarks. Don't be afraid to be silly and add a humorous spin to any conversation. Silliness is often the best way to make a point and can be a great way to make people laugh.

When you're out and about, don't be shy to comment. It can help break the ice and get people talking in a fun way. There's something incredibly satisfying about turning an ordinary situation into something more amusing.

Use Irony

Irony is a great way to add a humorous spin to any joke. It can be used to make a point or to poke fun at a situation. For example, you could use irony to point out the absurdity of a situation or to mock someone humorously. Irony can be used to make clever jokes and observations about everyday life. It's essential to remember that it should always be done for good fun - don't take yourself too seriously.

When using irony, paying attention to your tone of voice is necessary. This helps you convey the intended message in a lighthearted way without coming off as rude or offensive. Using sarcasm can be a great way to add humor to your jokes. But be careful, as overdoing it can come off as mean-spirited or even insulting; *tread carefully.*

When creating jokes, try to find the "funny" in the situation rather than relying on punchlines. This way, you'll create jokes that are more relatable and easier to understand. Remember to use puns! Puns involve swapping around words of similar sounds or meanings to create a joke or clever observation. It's essential to be careful with puns, as they can easily be misunderstood and come off as corny or cheesy.

It's great to be aware of the context when telling jokes. Even if you think a joke is funny, it may not be appropriate for the situation. Pay attention to your audience and keep their reactions in mind when crafting your jokes.

Be Creative

Creativity is essential for improvisation and comedy performance. While you don't need to be a genius to be a comedian, you must have an open mind and the ability to think outside the box.

Try creating unique takes on popular jokes or making up your jokes entirely. Don't be afraid to experiment - trial and error is the only way to become a better comedian. The more creative you are, the more likely you will come up with a joke that will get a laugh.

Avoiding Common Mistakes When Using Wit

Humor and charisma can be powerful tools when used correctly. The improper use of wit and charisma can have devastating consequences. To ensure that you make the most of your charisma, it's essential to properly understand how to wield humor and charisma in social settings.

1. Understanding the Social Context of Using Wit

Understanding the social context is the first step in avoiding pitfalls with your wit. Different situations call for different kinds of humor and charisma, and it's vital to be aware of this when engaging in conversation.

For example, a joke that may be perfectly acceptable at a party might not be appropriate in a business meeting. Understanding the social setting before using your wit can help you avoid potential pitfalls.

2. Avoid Being Too Self-Deprecating

While self-deprecating humor can often be funny, it can be seen as a sign of low self-esteem. It's vital to avoid using too much self-deprecating humor, as it can come off as negative and make you seem insecure.

A good rule of thumb is to use self-deprecating humor sparingly and only when appropriate. If you're unsure if a joke is too self-deprecating, err on the side of caution and don't push the boundaries too much.

3. Be Wary of Going Too Far

Remember that humor and charisma can be powerful tools but can backfire if you go too far. It's easy to get carried away in the moment and say something that offends someone or makes them feel uncomfortable.

To avoid this, always think before you speak and be aware of the reactions of those around you. If someone seems uncomfortable or if your joke is met with silence, it's best to just move on to another topic.

4. Memorizing Lines and Relying Too Much on Jokes

When using wit, avoid memorizing lines or relying too much on jokes. Memorized lines can be funny at the moment, but they often become stale quickly and make you seem like you've run out of original ideas.

It's essential to rely only a little on jokes, as this can make you seem one-dimensional. To ensure your conversations remain interesting and entertaining, use techniques such as storytelling, observational humor, and puns.

5. Know When to Hold Back

It's good to be aware of the mood of those around you. If you sense that your wit might not be welcomed in a particular situation, it's best to hold back and wait for the right moment. With a little practice, you'll soon develop the intuition and skill to recognize when your wit is welcomed and when it isn't.

Finally, remember that with comedy comes responsibility. As a wise person once said, "With great power comes great responsibility," and the same can be true with your wit. You can make any social situation more enjoyable and engaging with the right balance of humor and charisma. Just remember to use it responsibly!

Engaging in Clever Conversation

Bantering is a great way to express humor and build rapport with someone. Engaging in witty banter ensures that you understand the other person's sense of humor. Matching the other person's type of banter is vital, so you don't come off as out-of-touch or intrusive. Make fun of what you know about someone good-naturedly. Your remarks will only seem strong and intimidating if you use friendly body language.

You need to make sure that your comebacks have the right tone and amount of wit. Don't be too mean, but don't be too mild, either. Aim for a witty comment that will get a chuckle out of the other person, not an awkward silence. With some practice and creativity, you can become a master at making witty banter that will make any conversation more enjoyable. The key to making witty banter is to be yourself and have fun with it! Remember, the goal isn't to win an argument or prove you're smarter than the other person; it's just to enjoy some lighthearted banter and make the conversation more entertaining.

Humor and charisma can be powerful tools for making any conversation more enjoyable, and witty banter can be a great way to make those around you feel more at ease. It's essential to be aware of the boundaries of humor and ensure that what you say isn't inappropriate or offensive. If in doubt, err on the side of caution and keep your sense of humor lighthearted. With practice and confidence, you can become a master at witty banter.

Bonus: The Jokester's Checklist

Welcome to the bonus chapter! In this chapter, you will find additional hints and tips. However, these are based on the previous chapters, so certain sections may be like a movie recap.

As an additional bonus, we have provided you with a summary interwoven into this chapter's main topic, including all the tips given in the preceding chapters and an easy-to-follow checklist. This will help you track your progress on being funny and becoming a better storyteller, which will also improve your lifestyle in general.

Study the Art of Storytelling from Others

Mastering any craft requires a thorough understanding of what it entails, and the same is true for being a jokester. You should not simply rely on your initial thoughts and go out with the intention of being funny without observing the styles of others who have come before you. No one is going to laugh at your dry jokes.

You must watch and preferably attend comedy shows, clown parties, and other events guaranteed to make you laugh. It's common knowledge that success is never achieved in a vacuum. There were always people before you, and you likely found inspiration and motivation from one of them, just as there will be people after you.

There is more to creativity than just coming up with new ideas. A crucial part of creativity requires active listening, where you actively listen and comprehend the words and not just hear them. You need to pay close attention as other people tell stories so you can learn what works and what doesn't and how to engage an audience and keep them interested in what you're saying.

You must listen to what they say, how they say it, and watch their body language and facial expressions as they tell their stories in order to elicit the desired response from the audience: laughter!

Do not limit yourself to a single storyteller; the more storytellers you listen to, the more room you leave for your own creativity to flourish. Be humble and receptive to all suggestions, and do not hesitate to accept diverse viewpoints. When actively listening, jot down the things you deem significant and test them to find out which work best for you and which ones you should avoid.

There are also great authors in the field of comedy who have penned their secrets to success or a great piece from which you will learn a great deal. You may even read it multiple times. Reading is a great way to unleash your imagination, and it's also very entertaining.

Learn to Tell Thoughtful Jokes about Yourself

Your audience will undoubtedly feel at ease and find your story hilarious if your joke is not directed at them. In essence, you make fun of yourself, and your audience finds this humorous because they can let their guard down, and your stories are based on real events.

Even if the stories are not based on actual events, they are always funny when they are about the person telling the joke. Being funny requires you to have that essential quality of being able to laugh at yourself, either by saying or doing things that will be the ideal material for entertainment.

Unless you are an extremely good comedian, telling stories at the expense of others is unlikely to arouse laughter from your audience. You may be making it up, but the audacity of using them in thoughtless stories is not amusing, as they will see it as a mockery and could take offense.

Worse still, if you tell an embarrassing true story about a member of the audience in an attempt to be humorous, even if others find it amusing, it is a selfish act that can harm your reputation. One of the qualities that will work against you as a storyteller attempting to be humorous is telling stories that make you laugh at the expense of others - it can even put you in a very awkward situation.

Learn to Begin with the Right Hook

No one would wait in anticipation for the conclusion of a story that began in a boring manner, which is why it is essential to begin with a captivating hook. Although the storyteller's charisma must be magnetic, comedy does not depend solely on this quality. Your story's hook will attract your audience's attention and maintain their interest until the end.

Always begin your story with an intriguing sentence. Don't forget to spice it up with your tone, body language, and a dash of exaggeration. If you begin your story in this way, your audience will be eager to hear the conclusion. They'll be all ears; you don't want to ruin their excitement.

To make your story interesting, leave out tedious details and keep your audience's attention piqued from the beginning to the end with a strong hook.

This only highlights the significance of beginning with a good hook, the right one, to capture your audience's attention, keep them engaged with your dramatic displays, and reward them with a satisfying conclusion.

Maintain a Relaxed, Confident Presence

Now, you don't want to be cheesy when telling a story; otherwise, your audience will stop listening to you and instead focus on figuring out what's going on with you. Keeping your composure while you tell a story and appearing confident in your performance are two important aspects of being funny.

You must simultaneously learn how to maintain your composure during storytelling, feel at ease in your own skin and surrounding environment, exude confidence in every joke you tell, and make others laugh. While most people can maintain their composure by sipping water as they talk, others may find that pacing and avoiding eye contact work better.

Observe your surroundings and learn to read the room. Keeping track of how your audience responds to every word you utter will equip you with the knowledge to confidently adjust your story to the room's mood. If your audience is excited, you must match their energy and keep them excited. If they appear depressed, you are, of course, attempting to be amusing or make them laugh.

Consider yourself to be cool and think highly of yourself. Though you may only have control over yourself, your thoughts can profoundly impact those around you. Keep in mind that less is more, and practice saying no to suggestions that would derail your plans and schedule. Instead of concentrating solely on what you believe they should have, give some thought to what they actually want.

Ensure that you are a proactive narrator and not a reactive one and that your anticipations remain active. A proactive storyteller will always have backup plans in case their initial ideas fail, or there is an unexpected turn of events.

Being a reactive storyteller who can't predict changes can be taxing on a joke's setting, so it's important to be proactive to avoid having to keep retelling and blaming the past in the event that things don't go well.

Learn to Use Tone and Timing Effectively

Work continuously to improve your timing and tone. Your tone encompasses your style, voice, and context. It cannot be disputed that tone is a crucial component of comedy. Your tone gives your audience a glimpse into your story, and they can understand it even though you did not use any verbal words to explain it. Mastering how to deliver a joke with the appropriate tone and timing is something you should actively seek.

Sarcasm, when used correctly, can help you come across as funny. The sarcasm in your tone gives your context multiple meanings, making your story even funnier. A pause is sometimes necessary for good timing. Using a pause while telling a story will keep your audience interested and focus all attention on you. Pausing can also arouse your audience's anticipation for the next segment.

You will become a better storyteller if you apply the proper tone and timing to your expressions.

Use Body Language to Enhance Your Story

The way you move your body while you tell your story can either detract from or add to its impact. If you fidget, people will feel you lack self-confidence, which could be detrimental to your story. In contrast, when you tell a story while freely moving your body and including elements like raising your eyebrows, it enhances your story and keeps your audience interested in what you have to say.

People who are skilled at telling stories often use body language to enhance their performance, such as widening their eyes, holding a cold stare, and gesturing with their hands. Your audience can't help but pay attention to you when you use these kinds of theatrics because it stimulates their imagination and your artistic creativity.

Some storytellers use a lot of facial gestures, hand and leg movements, and even mime. Other storytellers communicate with their audience with expressive eyes matching the emotions in the story that is being told. They also use nodding and other neck responses.

You can use any body language hacks that you can confidently demonstrate to spice up your comedy and keep the laughter rolling.

Use Vivid Imagery to Bring Your Story to Life

Narrating a story is different from describing one. The reaction that you get from listeners in relation to a story that is narrated and the one that is described is also completely different. A good storyteller doesn't narrate a story. Rather, they describe each and every aspect of the story they tell.

The best storytellers use vivid imagery as a strategy that unlocks the effectiveness of the joke. This can leave the listener replaying the joke in his head, even after a long time has passed, and the action can be remembered.

Creating a vivid image for your audience to imagine enhances your joke and provides your audience with an actionable task.

Make a List of Foolproof Jokes

Some jokes in this book might not seem funny to certain people; always remain mindful that humor is subjective, so target your jokes appropriately! When uncertain, have a list of foolproof jokes handy; you may need them one day!

The success of your joke will be affected not only by the people who hear it but also by the environment in which it is told. Consequently, you need to be able to read people's feelings and the atmosphere and respond appropriately.

Improve Your Wit

You must have already understood the tricks and techniques that a storyteller can learn to make them funny and tell a good joke on the spot whenever required. You should have gained this understanding from all of the previous chapters. Given that you must tell jokes about yourself that are selfless and thoughtful, you must actually improve your charisma and wit.

The tips are not only for when you are on stage or in a setting where you are telling jokes but are for improving and maintaining the vibes in any type of conversation.

You can do other things to perfect your positive personal practices, such as watching as many sitcoms and comedies as possible or practicing telling jokes in front of a mirror.

You can also grow by getting out of your comfort zone once a week and talking to a stranger while attempting to make them laugh.

The Jokesters Checklist on How to Be Funny

1. Study the art of storytelling from others.
2. Learn to tell thoughtful jokes about yourself.
3. Learn to begin with the right hook.
4. Maintain a relaxed, confident presence.
5. Learn to use tone and timing effectively.
6. Use body language to enhance your story.
7. Use vivid imagery to bring your story to life.
8. Make a list of foolproof jokes.
9. Improve your wit.

Conclusion

Laughter is good medicine; a skilled storyteller can be like a pharmacist! The building blocks of a good storyteller are books, television shows, comedies, sitcoms, and gossip. You could also choose your storytelling style based on your favorite author and storyteller or a less-favorite one.

To become a great jokester, read as much as possible and practice active listening. This book has given you all the information you need to be able to drop a joke at any time that will make your audience laugh. It also offers tips on engaging your audience, maintaining the vibes in any conversation, and improving your wit. Furthermore, being open to opinions and suggestions will help you discover your style and what works best for you.

Witty people are exceptionally skilled at making others laugh with their clever and amusing jokes. One of the greatest assets is their ability to make spontaneous remarks about a person, a subject, or life in general. You can learn to be witty; over time, it will come naturally to you. Many people believe that good joke-tellers are intelligent, attractive, and insightful.

Even without making a sound, your facial expressions and hand gestures can elicit laughter from your audience. Other gestures such as nodding your head, twirling your neck, raising your eyebrows, and eye responses are actions that can enhance your storytelling by assisting your audience in visualizing what you are saying.

Aside from focusing on your listeners to give them what they want, a chapter in this book teaches you how to maintain your composure while looking confident and thinking of yourself as someone cool. Read your audience and the room's atmosphere and echo it in your stories.

Consequently, it is essential to begin with a hook that will captivate your audience from the outset, get them actively involved, and have them eagerly anticipate your conclusion. Along with the perfect hook, timing and tone are additional golden keys to a successful comedy. Tone consists of voice and style that provides your listeners with an understanding of the purpose of your speech. Using sarcasm and appropriate pauses are also successful secret humor techniques.

With body language and tone, you can etch a scene into the minds of your listeners that will have them reliving the moment and even laughing to themselves long after your performance is over. The vivid imagery will produce a generally compelling story that your audience will translate into their preferred realities.

Learning that the reception of a joke depends on both the audience and the environment demonstrates that the benefits of emotional intelligence are limited and that the context in which a joke is delivered must also be taken into account.

Finally, you can improve your joke-telling skills by reading up on literary devices like puns, irony, and sarcasm.

Tie all these concepts together, and you will be knocking 'em dead! Well, not really *dead*, but you get the picture. Best of luck in your humorous endeavors!

Here's another book by Andy Gardner that you might like

Free Bonus from Andy Gardner

Hi!

My name is Andy Gardner, and first off, I want to THANK YOU for reading my book.

Now you have a chance to join my exclusive email list related to human psychology and self-development so you can get the ebook below for free as well as the potential to get more ebooks for free! Simply click the link below to join.

P.S. Remember that it's 100% free to join the list.

Access your free bonuses here:

https://livetolearn.lpages.co/andy-gardner-how-to-be-funny-paperback/

References

ActiveLearningNetwork, P. by. (2018, May 14). "I'm all ears!" Active Listening as a tool for reflective thinking. The Active Learning Network. https://activelearningnetwork.com/2018/05/14/im-all-ears-active-listening-as-a-tool-to-reflective-thinking/

All ears: How listening can make you a better storyteller. (2017, June 29). Sinclair. https://www.sinclaircomms.com/insights/all-ears-how-listening-can-make-you-a-better-storyteller/

Fryer, B. (2003, June 1). Storytelling that moves people. Harvard Business Review. https://hbr.org/2003/06/storytelling-that-moves-people

Jenkins, P. (2021, September 3). Why Storytelling is Important for Culture. Brilliantio. https://brilliantio.com/why-storytelling-is-important-for-culture/

Ziegler, B. (2014, October 15). Listener as storyteller. Collaborativejourneys.com. https://collaborativejourneys.com/listener-storyteller/

Bitterly, B., & Brooks, A. W. (2020, July 1). Sarcasm, self-deprecation, and inside jokes: A user's guide to humor at work. Harvard Business Review. https://hbr.org/2020/07/sarcasm-self-deprecation-and-inside-jokes-a-users-guide-to-humor-at-work

(N.d.-b). Inc.com. https://www.inc.com/anne-gherini/what-a-self-deprecating-sense-of-humor-says-about-your-eq.html

How Transformational Leaders Use Self-deprecating humour. (2013, January 1). Ideas for Leaders. https://ideasforleaders.com/Ideas/how-transformational-leaders-use-self-deprecating-humour/

Self-depreciation: Why Do We Do It? (2019, April 2). Arcadia University. https://www.arcadia.edu/student-life/meet-our-students/cmcmullin/self-depreciation-why-do-we-do-it/

Alexandra. (2022, October 21). How to write a good hook that catches your readers' attention. SocialBee. https://socialbee.io/blog/how-to-write-a-good-hook/

Davis, S. (2022, July 15). 7 sensational essay hooks that grab readers' attention. Academic Writing Success - Master the Academic Writing Skills You Need to Succeed in School.

Lehman, D. E. (2022, April 28). The art of the hook. The Writing Cooperative. https://writingcooperative.com/the-art-of-the-hook-31b3c6657096

What is a narrative hook? (2022, December 31). Language Humanities. https://www.languagehumanities.org/what-is-a-narrative-hook.htm

[8 tips] how to be funny in conversation without trying too hard. (n.d.). Become More Compelling. https://www.becomemorecompelling.com/blog/how-to-be-funny

Knight, R. (2018, May 10). Tips for reading the room before a meeting or presentation. Harvard Business Review. https://hbr.org/2018/05/tips-for-reading-the-room-before-a-meeting-or-presentation

Managing conflict with humor - Helpguide.org. (n.d.). https://www.helpguide.org/articles/relationships-communication/managing-conflicts-with-humor.htm

Morin, D. A., & Viktor Sander B. Sc., B. A. (2020, January 21). 21 tips to be more fun and less boring to be around. SocialSelf. https://socialself.com/blog/be-more-fun/

Steve, E. (2022, May 7). How to be calm and confident? 11 Habits to be calm and confident. Stevewinroad. https://stevewinroad.com/how-to-be-calm-and-confident/

Walker, A. (2021, July 5). Five ways to be calm and confident every day. ESmartr Inc. https://esmartr.com/blogs/articles/five-ways-to-be-calm-and-confident-every-day

Andrews, M. (2013). Comic Timing. In Dickensian Laughter (pp. 50–76). Oxford University Press.

Kishore, K. (2020, September 7). Finding the right tone of voice in communication. Harappa. https://harappa.education/harappa-diaries/tone-of-voice-types-and-examples-in-communication/

Serious and humorous: Meaning & Examples. (n.d.). StudySmarter US. https://www.studysmarter.us/explanations/english/prosody/serious-and-humorous/

The humor effect: The benefits of humor and how to use it effectively. (n.d.). Effectiviology.com. https://effectiviology.com/humor-effect/

(N.d.-a). Masterclass.com. https://www.masterclass.com/articles/guide-to-comedic-timing

(N.d.-b). Backstage.com. https://www.backstage.com/magazine/article/comedic-timing-tips-75129/

Agrawal, H. (2016, May 15). 7 body language tricks to become likeable in the first meeting. Harsh Agrawal. https://harsh.in/body-language-tricks-become-likeable/

Laliberte, M. (2018, July 9). 9 body language tricks to get EXACTLY what you want from life. Reader's Digest. https://www.rd.com/list/body-language-tips/

Li, C. S. (2022, December 6). How to be funny: 7 easy steps to improve your humor. Science of People. https://www.scienceofpeople.com/how-to-be-funny/

Negru, H. (2016, June 12). 4 things you can learn from stand-up comedians about public speaking. Lifehack. https://www.lifehack.org/410724/4-things-you-can-learn-from-stand-up-comedians-about-public-speaking

Roye, S. (2022, September 11). Are you overlooking your most powerful laughter generation attribute? Top Stand-up Comedy Tips. https://www.realfirststeps.com/1008/body-language-biggest-laughter-generation-weapon/

Magher, M. (2014, April 4). How to create vivid imagery in your short story. The Classroom | Empowering Students in Their College Journey. https://www.theclassroom.com/how-to-create-vivid-imagery-in-your-short-story-12732447.html

Padhye, S. (2021, January 29). 10 techniques to improve your storytelling skills this year. Miracalize Media. https://miracalize.com/10-techniques-to-improve-your-storytelling-skills/

Practical Psychology. (2017, April 23). How to be Funny: 10 Tips to Improve your Sense of Humor. Practical Psychology. https://practicalpie.com/how-to-be-funny-10-tips-to-improve-your-sense-of-humor/

(N.d.-a). Masterclass.com. https://www.masterclass.com/articles/how-to-create-a-vivid-setting-for-your-story

(N.d.-b). Masterclass.com. https://www.masterclass.com/articles/how-to-write-vivid-descriptions-to-capture-your-readers

(N.d.-c). Masterclass.com. https://www.masterclass.com/articles/how-to-tell-a-story-effectively

Cars jokes. (n.d.). Upjoke.com. https://upjoke.com/cars-jokes

Geography jokes. (n.d.). Upjoke.com. https://upjoke.com/geography-jokes

Language jokes. (n.d.). Upjoke.com. https://upjoke.com/language-jokes

Literature jokes. (n.d.). Upjoke.com. https://upjoke.com/literature-jokes

Moore, H. (2004). Sports Jokes. Buddy Books. https://upjoke.com/sports-jokes

Nature jokes. (n.d.). Upjoke.com. https://upjoke.com/nature-jokes

Puns jokes. (n.d.). Upjoke.com. https://upjoke.com/puns-jokes

Rosenberg, P. (2012). Food Jokes. Child's World. https://upjoke.com/food-jokes

Ali, H., Mahmood, A., Ahmad, A., & Ikram, A. (2021). Humor of the leader: A source of creativity of employees through psychological empowerment or unethical behavior through perceived power? The role of self-deprecating behavior. Frontiers in Psychology, 12, 635300. https://doi.org/10.3389/fpsyg.2021.635300

Merolla, A. J. (2006). Decoding ability and humor production. Communication Quarterly, 54(2), 175–189. https://doi.org/10.1080/01463370600650886

Morin, D. A., & Viktor Sander B. Sc., B. A. (2019, November 8). 25 tips to be witty (if you're not a quick thinker). SocialSelf. https://socialself.com/blog/how-to-be-witty/

von Hippel, W., Ronay, R., Baker, E., Kjelsaas, K., & Murphy, S. C. (2016). Quick thinkers are smooth talkers: Mental speed facilitates charisma: Mental speed facilitates charisma. Psychological Science, 27(1), 119–122. https://doi.org/10.1177/0956797615616255

(N.d.). https://doi.org/10.1108/LODJ-11-2014-0231

Cuncic, A. (2013, August 30). How to be a better storyteller when you are socially anxious. Verywell Mind. https://www.verywellmind.com/how-to-be-a-better-storyteller-3024850

Lilley, K. (2018, August 10). Using Imagery In Storytelling is more than important for learners. ELearning Industry. https://elearningindustry.com/using-imagery-in-storytelling-important-learners

Morin, D. A., & Viktor Sander B. Sc., B. A. (2019, November 8). 25 tips to be witty (if you're not a quick thinker). SocialSelf. https://socialself.com/blog/how-to-be-witty

Printed in Great Britain
by Amazon

45144971R00066